Oppositional Defiant Disorder

A Parents' Guidebook for Children and Adolescents with O.D.D

MOMMY'S ANGELS
EDITORIAL STAFF
GROW YOUR TODDLER TO THE BEST!

ABOUT MOMMY'S ANGELS

GROW YOUR TODDLER TO THE BEST

Are you a first-time mother? Or are you planning for the arrival of your baby? Well, you are not alone on this exciting journey of your life. Of course, we understand that this period can be full of doubts and questions, which is why **MOMMY'S ANGELS** is a must-read for every young mother.

While you will have people around you who would want to help you, the surest way to understand what happens with your body, emotions, baby's health and everything related to pregnancy and even postpartum, is having a reliable personal guide by you 24/7 all-through the pregnancy period – whenever the need arises.

Although only you are going to feel what is happening inside you, the thought of having to filter through the countless books on pregnancy and parenting can sometimes be very daunting – especially during these forty weeks, the period of breastfeeding as well as the first few months of your baby. The **MOMMY'S ANGELS Series** include a vast range of book collections and vital tips that you need to help you grow your toddler to the best.

While these books are not intended to be a mandatory regime that you must follow, the comments, stories, and experiences of pediatricians, psychologists, gynecologists and other mothers like you, will help you enjoy the best adventure of your life.

Visit our various sections to find the best pregnancy books; including those for your toddlers and young children! You will certainly find the books very relevant and interesting, too!

Learn the most effective ways to grow your toddler with **MOMMY'S ANGELS Book Collections.**

MOMMY'S ANGELS
EDITORIAL STAFF
GROW YOUR TODDLER TO THE BEST!

Table of Contents

Introduction

Ground-Zero of the ODD Diagnosis

ODD symptoms will usually manifest in the home setting, and it's often the parents who seek professional intervention first. On rare occasions, the child's teacher or school administrator will be the one to suggest that the child be screened professionally.

If left unattended, ODD behaviors will cause the child to suffer socially, academically, and emotionally. Even if you've consulted the latest DSM manual, WebMD, and this book, don't attempt to diagnose your child on your own. If your child displays common ODD symptoms, take them to a psychologist or psychiatrist to obtain proper testing and diagnoses.

Fortunately, ODD is treatable, and with proper guidance, you can help your child improve and cope with the underlying factors that create this condition. There are also specialized training curriculums available for parents with ODD children. This training can be costly, but it can also be conducted in a group setting, which helps to lower costs while fostering social support. During these training sessions, you will learn different techniques that can be used to maintain clear-headed constructive control in various situations as they arise with your child. Family therapy is also, in some cases, an effective solution. In terms of medication, there are none tailored to this disorder. Research in this field is still new and ongoing.

Two Ways to Lessen Oppositional Defiant Disorder Behaviors

Next, we will cover some tips that you can implement today to gain back your control. You will not need extensive training to learn these simple, yet powerful tactics. Parents with individual children to teachers who want to cease behavioral distraction amongst all children in the classroom can find this useful. At times, the general atmosphere of the classroom or the way your child behaves is reflective of your mindset rather than children's negative behaviors. Strategies used to disarm one child's tactics can also be used as an example to show siblings or the rest of a classroom that they will not interfere with your day and state of peace.

Chapter 1 Interventions for Oppositional Defiant Disorders

Rapport Tonality

Plenty of authority figures talk to children who are defiant with a seeking rapport tonality instead of neutral/breaking rapport tonality. Speaking to children like they are children often goes unrecognized as a huge mistake. Let's dive into what's meant by that statement. The seeking rapport tonality is where the speaker's tone of voice will fluctuate upward toward the end of the sentence such as asking a question. You may also call it the "extra nice voice". Imagine how you would speak to your favorite celebrity if you met them minus the energetic excitement. Just focus on how your voice would sound when you speak. Now compare that tone to the way you speak with your students. Is the tonality similar? The breaking rapport tonality is where the speaker's tone fluctuates downward toward the end of a sentence such as a drill sergeant giving commands (without yelling). How does your boss speak to you? Do you speak to your students the way your boss speaks to you? The neutral rapport tonality is where your voice does not go too high or too low similar to when you

3

speak with close friends. Is this one similar to the way you speak with the child? Speaking in a calm, dominant, breaking rapport tonality when dealing with defiant children is most effective. At times, you may switch to neutral if you are trying to build comfort/connections which is highly important as well. Kids naturally respect you more if they feel like they can trust and relate to you. Both women and men can speak in a confident, breaking rapport tone. Adjusting your tone is not only important for compliance with children, but also essential to improving social skills which is why becoming aware of your habits is urgently important. If you are a natural people pleaser, the breaking rapport tonality may be difficult for you to hone. This analysis and readjustment will be a great opportunity to figure out the level of impact your tone is creating. The neutral and breaking rapport tones strongly enforce personal boundaries in an appropriate manner. The classic example given to explain the difference in tonalities is the boss-employee scenario. An effective boss can be polite, but their voice will rarely go up upward because they know that their status is higher than their employees. They are not trying to please them. Instead they're trying to lead while maintaining a certain level of respect and power. You attempt the same with children.

On the opposite side of the spectrum is the employee who tries to sound nice when interacting with their boss to avoid any trouble. Sometimes adults become fearful or avoid speaking in a demanding tone because they do not want to trigger the child. This is how seeking rapport tonality arises. That fear of triggering an oppositional defiant child forces a teacher to use their non-confrontational voice. Most people are not aware that something so simple can be tailored into a game-changing strategy. Here is a great *video* to further your understanding of this strategy and show you how to properly use your tone!

Using Leverage

Second, you want to use your leverage as an adult. Pay attention and figure out what makes your child light up and smile. Knowing what your child enjoys is important for using leverage. These are the privileges you will take away when threatening to put the child in timeout or on punishment. Common leverage you possess over a child is when they eat and sleep, the clothes they wear, presents received and the school they attend. You control their environment. Yes, they can ruin your day by becoming distractions, being annoying, and disrupting your state of mind. However, you have even more leverage because you have the power to take away their privileges. They cannot do the same to you. Most teachers, parents, and adults will yell at a child for hours upon hours repeating commands without ever giving any real consequences or following through with their threats. They solve the problem in short term with a quick chastising, but never take the time to teach the child important lessons about their mistakes (which will result in long term solutions). Most parents yell or give timeouts, then let the child return to their activities after a few minutes without telling them what they did wrong. The proper way to see behavioral changes with oppositional defiant children is to make them verbally the repeat plans of intervention after you lay them out. We will discuss this more in-depth in the next section.

Be sure to never argue with a child. Arguing gives them too much attention and kids can go for days. Working a behavioral health contractor in schools, I have watched countless teachers argue and tell a non-compliant child the same command over and over again. Yet, when I step in and tell the child to stop doing the same exact thing paired with the threat of taking away the child's favorite privilege, they will stop on the first command. In addition, I usually go up to the child's ear instead of openly talking and making a scene. Remember that defiant children who feel embarrassed in front on their peers will be emotionally triggered which results in greater defiance.

Once again, you have to know what your child enjoys in order to implement this strategy. Feel free to take away part of a privilege without taking it as a whole. Let's use chores and extracurricular activities as an example. Mike is a child with oppositional defiant disorder who likes to play basketball every day when he gets home after school. He loves basketball and you notice the pure excitement and fun displayed on his face every day when he shoots hoops with his friends. He is even very good at basketball and gets a lot of props from his peers on his talents. However, today Mike is not having a great day. He did not complete any chores, called you names, and told you "no" multiple times when you gave commands. He made the simplest tasks difficult for you today. You tell Mike that because he did not listen today, he can happily play outside, but he cannot play basketball. If you were to try to restrict the whole activity of going outside, it may make things stressful for you because you would have to watch him. Managing Mike while he is angry is extra work on your plate. You only need to take away the whole privilege if Mike touches a basketball. During this timeout when Mike constantly asks why he cannot play basketball, remind him of what he did wrong and how he can improve next time. You want to make sure children develop a habit of explaining what they did wrong and more importantly admitting what they did wrong, so they know not to do it again in the future. Again, you must do your part and hold up against excuses. Ignore any crying, complaining, or compromise as these are ways out of punishment for them.

Use Moments of High Intensity to Build Stronger Bonds

It's very important to build meaningful connections and strong bonds with a defiant child. This mission is not additional work. Speaking from observation, the most difficult children often are the easiest to love. They require so much attention that they take up all of your time investment. The more time you invest, the more you will grow to love wherever you spend your efforts. You can build stronger bonds through conversations about things you both enjoy, smiling, and doing fun activities together such as skating, taking an art class, dancing, or going out to an amusement park. Moments of high intensity when a child becomes triggered and may lash out is also a chance to build stronger bonds. For example, if a child becomes very angry because he was having an argument with another classmate and he ran out of the classroom, here's a good time to talk to the child in an intimate setting. Use this moment to express concern. Defiant children often feel as if the world is against them, so they adopt a victim mindset where nothing seems to be their fault. Remain sympathetic to their plight but also give valuable feedback.

Here is what you should say and how you should handle the situation above. Keep your distance and make sure the two of you have privacy. Let them express their anger, sadness, or other emotions freely. As they begin to calm down and remain still, you begin asking what happened and how do they feel. One of the first things I like to say is "I probably would have done the same thing you did" or "I feel the same way." You may tell a story from how you handled a similar situation in the past to build trust and relativity. This lets them know you have their best interest at heart and you want to help. Next, I discuss different scenarios of how the situation could have been handled better. If a child gets mad because another kid called them stupid, ask the child if they believe they are really stupid. Ask them if anyone in the school really knows them well enough to be able to judge them. Next, you want to get the child talking about what they will do next time to handle a similar situation better. Do not let them go until they verbalize their answer or repeat the advice you provided to solve the problem. For instance, if you want the child to listen on the first command, make them say, "I will listen on first command" before letting them off the hook. When we take ownership of words and speak them out loud, it sticks in our brains and becomes a part of our identity. This concept is related to affirmations. The more you speak a specific idea into reality, the more real it becomes and the sooner it will happen because it programs your subconscious mind to believe it. For instance, let's say name-calling is one of the child's triggers and they aggressively react by resorting to violence. To calm them down, you tell them that we all are called names at one point in our lives, but our reputation stays intact. Furthermore, iterate that they remain safe from physical harm because there is protection offered by adults and even by themselves. Ask them if they understand your message. Once the child confirms, make them repeat those sentences, preferably in their own words, to lock it in their psyche. This intervention will be imprinted in their train of thought the next time they are triggered. Eventually, the intensity of the reaction to the trigger will lessen.

In an intimate setting, a child does not have the pressure of their peers. There is no need to show off or uphold an identity as a "rebel." Children will often lash out in defiance in front of peers to avoid feeling embarrassed and losing their social status of power and respect with their peers. One-on-one conversations are calmer, and two people reach agreements faster. When is the last time you have seen or heard of two people fighting by themselves with no one else there? Fights happen when you add other people to the atmosphere. Tension arises as people try to make sure that their ego isn't being attacked and their reputation isn't damaged. Where there are witnesses, the stakes are high. People will do whatever it takes to stay on offense instead of defense. So, when your child is triggered, use this opportunity and shift into a compassionate counselor to help them recover and learn to optimize independence in their emotional battles.

Managing Stress, Having Compassion and Avoiding Burnout

Compassion fatigue is when you lose the desire to care about what you are doing as well as the will to want to help those people involved. Managing your stress as a parent with a defiant child can be frustrating, but it's up to you to be a leader. Keep your child in schools or child care services that are complementary to your current outgoing task of reshaping their behavior. In order to be a healthy parent, the child has to have an overall healthy environment to thrive. Settings that counteract your plans of intervention for triggers untangle and undo your hard work. Day after day you will have to restart with teaching an oppositional child how to manage their symptoms. Sending your child to an unorganized school with no good discipline or code of conduct takes twice as long to help nullify the symptoms of their disorder. Try to meditate, listen to music, go to therapy, or do something you find calming and relaxing to manage your compassion fatigue. Meditation is great because it gives your brain a chance to calm down from overthinking and enter a state of clarity. It allows you to be smarter and more effective about your interventions.

Chapter 2 How Acceptable Boundaries are Defined

As your child grows, they will already have had house rules pretty much covered and will know you as well as you know that child. However, the dynamics are not the same. Your child wants to be treated as an adult because they feel that they have earned that simply by living to the teen years. Their hormones are telling them that they are adults and this is a very awkward stage for teens since they want to be accepted by their peers and crave extra attention from people they care about – sometimes in a very defiant way to see how far they can manipulate the situation.

The Center for Parent and Teen Communication has set some guidelines for parents and these are very useful to know. Probably, a part of them forms part of your relationship with your child. However, you do need to read them through because there may be areas where you need to pay extra attention. Chances are that you have never parented teens or defiant children before and need to handle it in a better way, just like they haven't been the age they are and didn't know what to expect out of life.

One of the boundaries that they have set involves the way that you show your love for your children. A teen may reject the love that a younger child may crave, but they nonetheless need to know that regardless of the child's choices, that love is something a parent will always put first when coming up with any kind of boundaries and that the boundaries are there to keep that child safe. There have been parents who allow their children too much freedom, thinking it's a pretty cool thing to do, but really, can you expect a child of this age to take responsibility for actions you see as unacceptable, but they see as fun? The other side of this coin is that if you don't come up with boundaries, a child will push the edges of your sanity to see how he can win over whatever rules you decide to set up.

The Setting of Boundaries

There are several reasons for boundaries:

- Child privacy

- Parent's peace of mind

- Child's need to know what's right or wrong

There should also be consequences to going outside of those boundaries and it's a great idea to sit down with a child and talk these through. The reason this helps is that it isn't a parent dictating what's right and wrong, but a parent taking into account what the child's needs are and if these are viable, and what the parents expect of the child. Discussing with them, rather than dictating, helps them to help you to set the punishments for set actions before they happen, so there can be no question of bias once the punishment is served. Let your teen come up with graded punishments because then they'll see that they have some form of input.

As far as child privacy goes, it's hardly surprising that teens want more than children do. Their developing bodies are an embarrassment to them and they have not yet come to terms with the changes that happen to the body and the hormones during adolescence. Thus, teaching others to knock on doors before entering isn't a bad idea as one boundary to set. They may also want to know that their room is indeed their own safe place to be, and this can be established by telling the child that as long as the room is looked after and he treats it as a grown-up would, then their rights will be protected. It's very hard for parents to transition from looking after kids to looking after a defiant youth, but there are boundaries parents should never cross unless given due cause.

Similarly, there are boundaries which must always be enforced consistently when it comes to the rebellious teen. While they live in your family home, it's paramount that they understand what those boundaries are and that they take part in creating them. That way, there's no argument about implementing the necessary punishment, whether that is deprival of privileges or being grounded!

Negotiation

When you are teaching a child to be part of the grown-up world, it is vital that you let them know how much negotiation they are able to do with you. For example, if a child comes up with a suitable alternative to one of your boundaries, be open to listening. The idea is not to make the child feel that he or she is not being listened to, because that deepens rifts between parent and child, but negotiation helps them to become reasonable adults. Never feel that you have to give in to the demands of the child, but by the same token, allow the child's opinion to be listened to and considered as well as discussed, rather than simply playing the fool's card of "Because I said so."

It gives the wrong impression and it's quite likely that the child will take that kind of authoritarian attitude into their relationships with others. Your behavior toward that child has a legacy, so treat your child in a way that you want the child to remember for all of the good reasons when creating and negotiating boundaries.

Beginning With What You Can Control

Let's not kid ourselves. All parents get angry with their children. You get frustrated. You lose your patience. You say things you regret saying. You're not proud of it. You don't like to admit it, but when you've got stressors coming from work, spouses, or other children, and then you add an ODD child into the mix, things can spin out of control easily.

The great irony here is that when your child is suffering from ODD, it's even more important that you stay in firm control of your own emotions. If you, as a parent, resort to spitefulness, extreme negativity, or worse, physical violence, it will only confirm the validity of his behavior as an effective and normal means for getting what he wants. If you're raising an ODD child and have a tendency to lose your patience quickly, then you owe it to yourself to seek counseling. Regularly seeing a counselor will give you the time and space during which you and your needs will be the center of attention. Having this space could prove critical for a parent who's exerting an extreme amount of patience on the home front. Even if you're not having trouble controlling the expression of your emotions at home, raising an ODD child comes with a large amount of emotional wear and tear on the parent. It's perfectly acceptable, and encouraged, to seek professional support for yourself.

One of the mistakes parents make is waiting until an extremely significant, dangerous, or catastrophic event takes place before they seek professional help for themselves. If you believe your child may have ODD, then don't wait for an official diagnosis or for something bad to happen. Get support as soon as you can. Dealing with a child with ODD can be very stressful, and failing to find support results in putting you, your child, and the rest of your family members at risk. Caring for a child with ODD is going to be one of the most difficult challenges you'll ever take on. You have to be in top form, and a good therapist will help you get there.

There are numerous therapists' practices, programs and classes that cater to people looking to manage stress and anger. Therapy sessions, though often effective, can also be expensive. A cheaper alternative is anger management classes, where a group of people share individual experiences and offer tips and ways in which each member of the group successfully addresses anger-related issues. As long as you're actively building solutions for better self-control and also accessing a human support network, you're going to be in a much better position, emotionally, to take on the challenge of an ODD child.

Parents who are able to control their emotions when dealing with an ODD child are able to subtly establish leadership in the relationship. You may not be able to control what your child says or does, but you can show him how problems can be resolved in a calm and civil manner. Failing to keep composure and giving in to anger can result in you losing both your self-respect and all credibility with your child.

Let's consider the plight of a Rhonda, from Thousand Oaks California. Rhonda's story— though based on an actual situation involving a Southern California woman raising an ODD child—has been altered slightly to protect her identity. Rhonda's teenager, Jacob, had such extraordinary anger that he would regularly sneak up behind his mother and grab her by the neck and pretend, quite convincingly, to choke her when he was in a foul mood. This was a bizarre, dangerous behavior and one of many ODD symptoms that Jacob exhibited. Having been expelled from his high school for physically assaulting a teacher, Jacob spent countless hours with his Xbox, playing violent shoot-em-up video games. He refused to do any work around the house and maintained a consistent attitude of disrespect and anger towards both his father and mother. Jacob's father, Clint, had always been the more passive and dismissive parent when it came to Jacob's behavior. Clint's softer, deferential approach to handling Jacob seemed to feed Jacob's anger. Meanwhile, Rhonda, feeling unsupported by her husband in the midst of an incredibly trying situation, was on the brink of filing for divorce. Rhonda had come from an abusive home, with an alcoholic father who couldn't contain his own anger. Seeing shades of her own father in Jacob, who, at 17, was also prone to abusing alcohol and drugs, left Rhonda in a state of despair. And then, one day, she lost control.

It happened during one of Jacob's tirades, apparently the result of becoming frustrated by a video game. Jacob stormed into the living room and kicked Junior, the family's golden retriever. The dog yelped. Rhonda, aghast, screamed at him, "Jacob!"

"Fuck off," was his prompt and snide response.

Before she knew what she was doing, Rhonda slammed her son up against the wall and struck him repeatedly with flailing arms, elbows, and fists. Jacob was so stunned by the behavior that he didn't even attempt a violent response—quite uncharacteristic for him—but wriggled away from his mother's assault and screamed at her, "You crazy bitch!" before retreating back into his room behind a slammed door.

Some parents' violent reactions arise from deeper issues, rooted in their own childhood. We all enter parenthood with wounds, and some of us, like Rhonda, have been more deeply traumatized than others. The ODD child has a way of unknowingly opening up your old wounds, which in turn spurs forth impulses to negative reactions. Sometimes your knee-jerk responses are so deeply ingrained in your psyche that you barely have a chance at controlling yourself. Such negative reactions can harm the child, and eventually may even shape his future with his own children. This cycle of emotional baggage, and abuse, can continue indefinitely across multiple generations.

Sounds like quite a dire outlook, but let's see if there is a bright-side to all of this. As a parent of an ODD child, you're inevitably going to be put in a situation where your own baggage is brought to the surface. But now you're dealing with your issues as an adult and have more control over what happens to you and more awareness with regard to how to process these feelings that you've not felt since your own childhood. If you think about it, this is an incredible opportunity for you.

A pessimist sees the difficulty in every opportunity; an optimist sees the opportunity in every difficulty.

- Winston Churchill

The challenge you're facing in dealing with an ODD child, when optimistically contextualized, is a chance to break a deeply, perhaps genetically, ingrained destructive cycle. Every step you take towards breaking this cycle, including reading this book, should be considered a heroic act.

So now that we have established the dangers of resorting to anger-motivated responses to your child, here are some ways in which you can keep your anger in check:

Know When Too Far is Too Far

Understanding your limits is one of the best ways to keep your anger in check. When we angrily go after our children, it is usually because we haven't set limits for ourselves when it comes to how we intend to deal with our children. It's important that these personal, self-controlled limits are established and abided by consistently. Some parents, for example, determine that they will never discipline their children by spanking but by confiscating coveted possessions, or rewarding good behavior. Other parents decide that spanking is okay, as long as it's not undertaken while the parent is angry.

There's no perfect parenting philosophy, and different approaches work with different children. But most parents and psychologists agree that consistency and boundaries are important. To help you reflect on and clearly define appropriate limits for discipline, sit down and create a list—use a note-taking app on your phone, or even use a Post-It sticker—of disciplinary measures that are acceptable, and those that are never permissible. Read over your limits on a regular basis. Remember, these limits may not be intuitive to you, especially in the heat of anger, as you may not have been raised in a household where such limits were applied.

If you're instinctually inclined to express anger, don't feel bad about it. It's perfectly normal. You just need to find an alternative channel to vent through. Make another list and write down ways that you can deal with anger and the other negative emotions that are inevitably going to arise as you struggle to deal with your ODD child. Some ideas may include: going for a walk, playing some calming music, meditating, or just locking yourself in your room for a while and taking some personal time. It's also, as previously mentioned, helpful to have a counselor to talk to.

Recognize and Prevent False Alarms

When you're dealing with a child that constantly presses your buttons, you may, at times, find yourself inclined to blame things on him or her, even when it's not warranted. Many times, as a parent, you'll see your child doing something questionable, or out of the ordinary, and you'll instantly become upset or angry about it. "Cut it out," you'll say to a child who's adding enthused audio commentary to the drama unfolding in his Lego set. He's just a child playing with Legos, but in your mind, for a split second, he's being unruly, and you want him to knock it off.

At times like these it's helpful to take an introspective moment. Perhaps you're irritable because you've had a rough day at work, or maybe you've got a headache, and your child is annoying you just by being, well, childish. Misplaced anger is a phenomenon present not only in parent-child relationships, but in several other social settings. It's especially critical to be aware of your behavior and potential misplaced anger when dealing with an ODD child, because you've likely become so habituated to scolding your child that it's become second nature.

Not only will you feel badly if you go off on your child when they don't deserve it, but you will also adversely affect any efforts your child is making to improve their behavior. When you're inclined to scold your child after a rough day at work or after a trying event, stop and reflect for a minute on what's really irritating you. If the child's behavior truly requires discipline or correction, then simply approach your child as you would normally, in a calm and controlled manner. Remind them of the rules that have been established. Phrase your instruction by letting your child know what you need from them — I need you to etc. This phrasing puts your child in a position of feeling important, and will make them feel valued.

Don't be cynical and think that just because your child is ODD that they don't care at all about pleasing you. Your child cares, but often believes that it's not possible, so they succumbs to despair, anger and helplessness. Tell your child exactly what they can do to please you and address them with a firm calmness. You may be surprised at your child's responsiveness.

Isolate Yourself

This may be the most effective means of letting go of your anger. When you are separated from the source of the problem, then you will be able to let go of your anger more quickly. Isolate yourself by locking yourself in the bathroom or the bedroom, and count to ten, listen to music, read a book, or pray. Do whatever you need to do to keep your emotions under control. When you have calmed down, you can return to dealing with your child.

Avoid Reacting Physically

If your aim is to maintain a clear, calm, and controlled response when dealing with your ODD child, then you should strive to avoid spanking. Spanking can easily escalate to more damaging whippings and beatings, especially when dealing with an ODD child. If you must spank, always do so at least 15 minutes after the incident has taken place. Make sure that you're not spanking while fueled by anger and adrenaline.

Though spanking is used as a disciplinary tool in over 80% of American homes (according to the American Academy of Pediatrics), it's come into strong disfavor among psychological professionals. In Irwin A. Hyman's groundbreaking, The Case Against Spanking, Hyman notes how one of the most appalling practices of white settlers, as observed by native Americans in the 15th and 16th centuries, was hitting of children by parents. Though it's deeply ingrained in our culture, it's not necessarily an optimal approach to discipline.

You may resort to physical punishment because it was used to discipline you when you were growing up. When considering the use of corporal punishment, as an adult, in your own household, it's important to reflect on the feelings of low self-worth that you may have experienced in your own childhood. These are the feelings commonly associated with being spanked or whipped as a child.

Many parents are inclined to refer to their having, "turned out fine," when they want to justify spanking, and even whipping (the repetitive striking of a child with a hairbrush, whip, or similar tool). In actuality, no one is fine. You carry some emotional scarring, regardless of whether you were spanked or not, regardless of whether you've enjoyed healthy adult lives or not. Surviving any kind of abuse does not justify the abuse. Learning to discipline without spanking can break a chain of emotional scarring, especially when it comes to dealing with ODD children, who need more than anything, positive examples of how problems can be resolved without resorting to anger and violence.

Unfortunately, physical punishment on an ODD child usually results in more resistance, more defiance of authority, and generally more acting out in inappropriate, aggressive, hostile, and violent ways.

Consider Better Methods for Disciplining Your Child

So, if you can't yell or spank a child with ODD, then what can you do? Punishing a child, though necessary, is always going to be a form of negative reinforcement. The best ways to punish will equate the negative reinforcement with the lack of a positive reinforcement or reward. One idea you can try is the use of allowances.

Allowances are privileges the child receives that are contingent on cooperative behavior. Once the child ceases to be cooperative, then the allowance is revoked. In Rhonda's case, seeing how her ODD teenager, Jacob, loved to play video games, using his access to the video game console or television would have served as the perfect allowance. When Jacob behaved disrespectfully or refused to do his assigned chores, his video game privileges will be taken away.

When setting up an allowance system for your child, be sure to take the opportunity to sit down and discuss how the system is going to work with them. You want to be perfectly clear about what's expected of the child and what the consequences will be for their failure to fulfill the expectations. Prepare yourself, an ODD child will object to every aspect of your proposal. You have to trust that the system you're laying out is fair and stick to your guns. Don't let your child bait you into an argument or debate.

An ODD child will thoroughly test your resolve to stick to your allowances program. They will feel out any vague or gray area of your set-forth requirements and exploit it relentlessly. If part of your child's responsibility is to sweep the driveway once a week, be prepared for them to make a half-hearted and incomplete effort. How are you going to respond? If your child is required to study for at least an hour every evening, how are you going to ensure that they do so? If you have a parenting partner, sit down with him or her and think through every dimension and contingency of your plan, then execute it.

Privately Empathize with Your Child's Predicament

One way in which you can maintain your equanimity and reign in the impulse to anger, is by thoughtfully and regularly putting yourself in your child's shoes. If your ODD child is still very young, imagine how it might seem threatening when someone, three times bigger than them, tells them they're doing something wrong. Because of their disorder, your child has trouble trusting and deferring to your guidance and instructions and the only response that makes sense to them is emphatic resistance.

Brain scans have shown that the brains of children with ODD have key neurological differences in the areas which control impulsivity and judgment. Even though your child may not be telegraphing that they're afraid and confused and unsure of themselves, that's very likely exactly what's going on inside your child's mind. Your child may see you as a lightning rod, there to absorb all of their angst and resentment towards a world they don't understand.

When you show anger while dealing with your ODD child, this leads them to identify an area in their life where their influence and power is truly felt and your child will continue to provoke you so as to feel that level of control and importance again. No, you can't control everything as a parent, but you can control some things. You can control the way you respond to a challenging predicament and when dealing with a child with ODD, your best approach is staying in control of yourself. This means remaining calm, communicating clearly, disciplining in a consistent fashion with clear limitations drawn, and finding constructive, safe ways to deal with your own natural anger.

Chapter 3 Problems at School and/or At Home

Some children have behavior problems that only surface at home, some only at school, and others in both settings. In the majority of cases, implementing this program at home is sufficient to affect school behavior as well. Children's home environments provide templates for how they behave elsewhere, so learning to respond to parental limits creates a process that gets internalized and then echoes into the school.

PROBLEMS MAKING OR KEEPING FRIENDS

As young children leave home and attend school, a primary source of their self-esteem comes from how peers relate to them. Children who aren't sufficiently connected to friends become unhappy, especially by third grade. All too frequently, kids who have problems responding to limits at home also have trouble making and keeping friends.

The reason? These kids haven't learned to be sufficiently attentive to others' needs. Simply put, they don't share very well. It's not just about sharing your cookie or taking turns, but something equally important—what we call "sharing influence." Because they have had too much power at home they tend to want to be in charge too much with their peers. This turns other kids off.

As children learn to be better behaved and less self-absorbed, then and only then can they interact with friends in ways where they share influence. Learning consideration for others allows them to say things like "How about let's do what you want first, and then I get to choose."

ACTING OUT ONLY IN SCHOOL

There are a number of reasons that kids can be acting out in school and not at home. Some factors relate to things that are happening at school, such as being bullied, socially isolated, or having special education needs that aren't being met.

Yet another explanation for kids' misbehavior in school is how things are going at home. There are two different patterns that are typical:

One pattern is that a child is being treated too punitively at home. Kids can be afraid of their parents, upset about how they are being disciplined, but instead of expressing their upset at home, they carry their anger and defiance into the classroom or playground. When parents are using spanking, yelling, or physical forms of punishment with strong emotion, kids often act out these same behaviors. This is a case of monkey see, monkey do.

Other kids may act out in school because there is too much tension in the family. Sometimes mom and dad are fighting, sleep-deprived, or stressed out about work or health conditions. These children, especially sensitive ones, are typically acting out and expressing their stress and upset at school. The following case example illustrates this:

-

A mother and paternal grandmother were raising a seven-year-old girl named Grace. The friction in the room was palpable as these two parenting figures met in my office for the first time. They were at odds with each other about how and whether to set limits with Grace, who hadn't been completing homework, was getting into trouble with playground teasing, etc. It took a few sessions to help the adults work out their accumulation of upsets and resentments with each other. Then, and only then, could they team up and be on the same page about discipline. When the adults were able to collaborate and follow through with appropriate limits, Grace settled down.

Regardless of the specific family patterns that may be contributing to a child's misbehavior, the Win-Win Way is effective. As kids become less anxious and upset, they are less likely to act out in anger. They learn limits at home and their better behavior generalizes into the classroom. In a very caring fashion, you want your children to feel loved without giving them the message that they are the center of the universe.

Who Are They, Anyway?

In previous generations, if children obeyed their parents, it was typically out of fear of a spanking (or worse), a guilt trip, a public shaming, or any number of aversive approaches. Congratulate yourself if you haven't had to resort to these old ways. But today's parents face a new dilemma. If your child isn't afraid of you and doesn't really care so much about what you think, you're in a bind. Now what do you do? You don't want to spank but don't have other strategies to replace the old ones. You may want to be more in charge but don't know how to get there from here.

As therapists, we get a high number of referrals of defiant, strong-willed children from pediatricians, teachers and principals. These kids already carry pretty heavy labels such as Oppositional Defiant Disorder and Bipolar Disorder. Parents will typically ask that their child be seen in individual therapy. Parents, and many professionals, as well, still haven't figured out that problems rarely exist only inside a child. It is the context of a child's life that can bring out the best or the worst. The primary context for young children is their home life— how they are being loved, cared for and disciplined.

This is why we work with parents from the outset. How can we "fix" a child without including the most important, powerful influences in that child's life? If you think about it, isn't it silly to imagine that an hour a week, even with an excellent therapist, will be more effective than changing the quality of a child's interactions at home? If after we teach parents this new approach, their kids change dramatically in a few weeks, is that because the disorder has been eradicated? Clearly not. The context in which the problem emerged has been turned around to bring out the best.

Any successful program with young children needs to emphasize the incentives and consequences for the child either behaving or not behaving. Raising your voice, scolding, repeating yourself and lecturing kids lets them know what you want, but these actions don't necessarily impact your child. From our experience, these strategies simply don't work very well. You may want them to behave in a certain way, but unfortunately they don't necessarily care about it just because you do.

Did you ever use "reverse psychology" when your kids were little? Did you ever say, "No, no, don't eat your spinach!" to your two-year-old and see them giggle hysterically as they eagerly shoveled it down? This same strategy can work with older kids as well. Kids who are commonly labeled "spirited," "strong-willed" or "stubborn" are ripe for this approach. In fact, playfully telling a child not to do something, or at least giving them a real choice— that's when the magic begins.

The trap that many parents fall into is caring more about how their child is behaving than the child does. The more that parents push their kids to behave, the more the child pushes back. These efforts usually backfire and create a counter-reaction. This makes sense from the standpoint of developmental psychology because kids in the 3 to 10-year-old age range are naturally differentiating from their parents as they become their own persons. It's part of growing up. The idea of using reverse psychology, particularly with the star chart that we will describe, will be a key element of your success.

TESTING, TESTING 123

Strong-willed kids who are acting out essentially have two different competing "sub-selves" operating. One self is saying "I'm the boss and I want to run the show and do whatever I can get away with. Just do what I want all the time, everything will be fine, thank you very much!"

The other sub-self, that they may be less aware of, feels guilty and bad for getting away with so much. When kids have too much power, they become anxious and keep searching to find clearer boundaries. They have more power than they can handle. Therefore, the best way to conceptualize a child's misbehavior and defiance is that the child is testing. Like the old country-western lyrics "Looking for love in all the wrong places," we often quip that these kids are "looking for limits in all the wrong places."

The best way to describe and define your child's strong-willed and out of control behavior is that they are testing you. Kids thrive when they are provided with appropriate limits. In fact, they will continue to test, push, shove and prod until you respond appropriately and provide a safe container for their behavior and impulses. The challenge then, is how to provide these boundaries and structure in a way that is not only caring and respectful, but also effective.

Reducing Negative Emotions

By the time most parents seek psychological help, they have typically tried a number of fairly unsuccessful strategies for getting their children to behave. The common thread is the high level of frustration that happens when a child basically ignores you.

It's normal to have lots of big feelings—fear, anger, hurt—when your child is misbehaving. One of the most upsetting moments is when your kid is "in your face" with defiance, and one of the most common traps parents fall into in these moments is to yell at them.

It can really push your buttons when you feel disrespected and ignored. Funny thing, but your kids don't consider all the ways that you've sacrificed yourself for their benefit. Inside, if you're honest with yourself, you're probably thinking "I break my butt to provide you with your toys and privileges and the life that you have, and here you are, you ungrateful little ****, not listening to me when I'm simply asking you to brush your teeth!" Although very normal, this feeling of outrage can create overwhelming guilt in loving parents.

An essential element of the Win-Win Way is to parent without a lot of emotional upset. The existence of mirror neurons in the brain makes clear the disadvantages of angry parenting.

WHY MIRROR NEURONS MATTER

An important discovery from the world of neuroscience and brain imaging is the existence of mirror neurons, first seen in monkeys and later found in humans. Whenever we are observing someone else, our mirror neurons fire, mimicking in our brains what is going on in the brain of the other person. Emotions are contagious! When we see emotions in another's face, we immediately sense that same feeling in ourselves. This discovery helps us to understand why children learn through imitating and how empathy is wired in biologically.

When it comes to families, mirror neurons have important implications. We are constantly impacting and being affected by the mood states of those around us. Haven't you had the experience of feeling perfectly fine, then meeting up with your husband or wife who looks angry or upset only to have them ask why you are upset with them? Now we know that a subtle unconscious dance is going on behind the scenes. Although misery may not love company, misery finds company quickly when the mirror neurons fire. Equally true, if you yawn or get the giggles, you are sure to be joined by people around you.

Because kids reflect our emotional states, our parenting anger gets recycled back into the family in a never-ending downward spiral. Without warning, the hurricane blows in. Negative emotions escalate into mean words and actions we later regret. "NO SCREEN TIME FOR THE REST OF THE WEEK!"

Some kids express their anger immediately and directly. They hit, kick, or say things like "I hate you!" or "You're a terrible mom." Other kids express their anger indirectly or passive-aggressively by taking their sweet time when we need them to get in the car and off to school. Alternatively, their anger can get directed at siblings, peers, a family pet or at school. Sound familiar?

TOOLS TO HANDLE YOUR OWN ANGER

Now that we've established the importance of lowering negative emotions in the family, here are some tools to help you parent more calmly. There are two different methods of handling upsets, each useful in a different way. We recommend that you practice both:

Expressing your feelings on your own in a constructive manner.

Using methods of deep breathing and centering to calm you down.

EXPRESSING FEELINGS CONSTRUCTIVELY

Expressing feelings in constructive ways helps heal our bodies, relationships, and families. Rather than trying to hold feelings of anger when your child is pushing all your buttons, it's best to let them out, but not by yelling at your child.

-

A precautionary note: Although the methods we describe can be useful for people with a history of explosive anger, sometimes more is needed. It is essential to find means of expression that are not hurtful to others. If this is too difficult to accomplish on your own, be sure to seek professional help and guidance.

METHODS OF CALMING

Below are several methods to calm emotions. Ideally you will apply them at the earliest moment you realize you are upset.

Simply walk away from the situation and give yourself some space.

Take some long, slow deep breaths. Make sure to fill your lungs up completely and breathe out the tension as you exhale.

Some people like to close their eyes for a few moments. Splashing your face with water can also have a calming effect.

If you have the ability to either look out a window or walk outside, try having a brief encounter with nature.

Rather than just focusing on the crisis moments, it also helps to take preventative measures of reducing stress. Practice some form of self-calming at least once or twice daily when you're not on the firing line. People don't think twice about routinely brushing their teeth. If you practice self-relaxation or meditation for five minutes twice a day for the rest of your life, you will be more able to successfully calm your emotions when you need to do so quickly.

USING THE COMBO

We recommend that you experiment with all of the methods described above, seeing what works best for you. In our experience, however, using both of the general strategies works best. For any given circumstance that really upsets you, try expression first and calming methods second—for example, screaming in a pillow and then quieting yourself before interacting with your child. Don't worry that you'll have to be escaping to another room to scream in a towel for the rest of your parenting days. After a few weeks of practice, most parents no longer need to express as much, especially because levels of stress have fallen so dramatically after implementing all of the methods of the Win-Win Way.

AIM FOR DETACHMENT

From the standpoint of human dynamics, one of the most significant problems for families with kids out of control is that the parents care how their child is behaving, but the child cares very little. What can work better for you, paradoxically, is to learn how to operate from a psychological space where you don't care so much. Of course, you care immensely about your child but you need to be less devastated or upset by the acting out behaviors. See them as calls for love and limits. This new insight fosters the detachment you need to parent calmly and effectively. The goal is to help kids want to behave for reasons other than just because you want them to.

With this model, you are simply providing incentives and consequences for behavior so that your child has increased motivation to cooperate. Here are some examples of ways we suggest that you give your child a choice to comply or not.

"Nathan, would you like to pick up your toys like I asked, or would you rather spend some time in the corner?"

"Samantha, you can either hand me the iPad right now, or would you like me to take it away for an hour?"

"Juniper, do you want to stop talking to me like that or shall I take away some time from your TV tonight?

No big drama, no standing over the child, no attachment (as in being attached or driven to get a certain outcome). If you have an investment in things being a certain way, kids will simply rebel. The paradox is that the more you don't care how your child behaves and simply let the consequences work, the more your child will start to care and step up to the plate.

Imagine that a police officer pulls you over for speeding. He doesn't warn you, scold, lecture, guilt trip, hit you or repeat himself. He just gives you a ticket. And if that's not enough to do the trick, the subsequent one costs even more. Although we don't want to play cops and robbers, the use of appropriate consequences prepares our kids for the real world.

Chapter 4 Your Superhero Role

Can you put your role or job description as a parent in writing?

Is it to protect your children?

Is it to make them happy?

Is to lavish them with attention?

Make them feel loved?

All of the above?

I'm positive that you would choose to protect your children from harm, lavish them with attention, and keep them happy. But, is that your role in your children's lives?

Let's look to nature for a moment...

Imagine if all the bunny rabbits in the world suddenly decided to lavish their offspring with attention, protect them from predators, and go out of their way to make their young happy...

What would happen to them once they became adults and their parents were sick of tending to their every need? Would they have the skills to survive on their own?

We all know that the answer is a big fat "NO!"

The one thing missing in nearly every single parenting book and article we have found is that our role for our children is to prepare them for life. The only one that comes close to explaining the importance of teaching our children how to master their emotions is Dr. Leonard Sax's book, The Collapse of Parenting.

We don't owe our children cable television, wifi and cell phones; we owe our children a set of life skills including morals and virtues like responsibility, respect, focus and self-control.

We know this intuitively.

We teach our babies to:

Hold a fork

Walk when the time is right

Get up and keep trying even though they continue to fall down

Go to the bathroom on their own

Get a glass of water — hopefully.

If they want a drink, they know that life skill and can get it on their own. If they don't know how, it's up to you to teach them.

You can easily find parenting experts offering parenting tips like "Get down on your child's level and speak in an authoritative voice."

But, is this really going to help your child learn how to get what's important to them in a solution-oriented and proactive way?

Focusing on solutions for temper tantrums, rebellion and anger is a backward way of thinking. It places the child as the cause and the parent's reaction as the effect. This also puts the child in a leadership position. It matches nature's law of cause and effect in an extremely frustrating way for all.

We speak with new parents every day who share that they are desperate for answers dealing with unruly child behavior. The natural habit is always "What do I do when my child does this?" It's reactive. It's like jumping out of an airplane without a parachute and then asking, "What do I do now?"

Psychology Today says that emotions override rational thought. There's no way to be logical with an angry adult, let alone an angry child.

This is a perfect scientific equation for negative results like:

Anger

Anxiety

Depression

Chaos

Broken relationships

Misunderstandings

Miscommunication

A hundred other negative emotions and circumstances.

If this is what you're after, following your current parenting style has you right on track!

Here's the formula for a toxic home or class environment:

Child's Ignorant Action + Parent's Angry Reaction = Stress Effect.

Most of society is focused on today's poor child behavior from an adult perspective. We are not taking the time to teach them in advance what their expectations are.

Dr. Leonard Sax shares an interesting passage in his book, The Collapse of Parenting. "When his parents didn't buy him the toy he wanted, he would scream in the toy store. But his parents had never taught him the rules of good behavior. His behavior was pretty much what you would expect of a kid who has never known consistent discipline."

He is confirming that the boy has a habit of crying in the store because it's worked for him in the past. Instead of consistent discipline, however, we would look at consistent practice showing him how to get a toy when he goes to the store rather than be in a position of a yes or no answer.

We tend to know this in our business lives or at our jobs.

Can you imagine showing up for your first day of work not knowing at all what to do? Everyone assumes you do. Every time you go to make a move, they yell at you.

"No, we don't do that!"

"Stop it!"

"Shut up!"

"Don't touch!"

Would you now know what to do? How long would you choose to work in that environment?

Now, what if you were stuck there? You have no choice but to live in this dictatorial and unproductive, hellish environment. How happy could you possibly feel?

You're right! You couldn't feel happy at all.

Here, let me draw it out for you again.

Worker's Ignorant Action + Boss's Angry Reaction = Frustrated Effect.

Here's an example of reactive parenting:

It's a beautiful afternoon. You don't want to be cooped up on such a nice day with screaming kids who constantly bug each other. Deciding it would be fun to take your small children for a walk to the park, you excitedly announce the idea to your children and walk over to turn the television off.

"Okay, let's get our jackets and shoes on so we can go for a walk to the park," you dictate cheerfully. You finally get to enjoy some fun with your little love bunnies!

Your cheerful demeanor begins to dissipate as confusion and anxiety set in.

Your children don't seem as excited about going for a walk as you are. They are upset that you turned the television off. In an attempt to avoid a power struggle, you successfully distract them. You turn their attention to the great outdoors. Phew...meltdown averted! Yay!

You gather your little ones up and head out the door to the park...hoping your outing is fun and worth the effort.

Before you know it, your children are happily running up and down the sidewalk.

But, you've been here before, or you've heard a story. You begin to feel worried.

Fear begins to cause an alarm to go off inside your mind. As annoyed as you are with your toddlers, you love your children greatly. You want them to be safe.

You begin to yell, "Hey, little Timmy, come back to Mommy!"

Now your younger child, who's two, thinks you're playing a game. He begins to run further away. Your worst nightmare is actually happening! You yell louder. As your panic heightens, he seems to be running faster and faster directly towards the busy street ahead.

You throw everything to the ground! You are in a mad rush! All you can think about is catching him before he gets to the main road and hit by a car!

Your toddler is giggling. He appears to be laughing at you, which causes you to become angry.

You don't want to experience this again. Ever! Never!

You reach him just as he approaches the street.

You yell at him.

You spank him!

You make him feel bad so he can relate the bad feeling to the experience.

You believe you are teaching him so you can protect him.

All the while, your toddler knows nothing of the danger on the streets. From his point of view, he was simply playing with you. He trusted you to show him the ropes and to be on his side.

In an attempt to protect your baby from danger, you unknowingly wound his soul. It is a wound you cannot see, but it is there. A wound that will last forever.

Does this sound familiar?

It's like parenting today is in constant reaction to poor child behavior. It's causing most moms, especially North American moms, to live in a continuous state of stress and frustration.

Maybe your child doesn't run on the streets. Perhaps they yell or run in the house.

What is your go-to statement for when your children are doing something you don't like?

Do the statements you use absolutely show your child exactly what you want them to do?

With all that being said, if you begin lecturing your child on the way the world works, will they really get what you're saying? Can your child fast forward their mind and know what it's like to be an adult?

If you have a goal to raise healthy, happy, cooperative kids, all you need to do is become the cause with a proactive plan for your child and teach them in advance!

Antoine de Saint-Exupéry, a famous 1930s children's book author and philosopher, said, "A goal without a plan is just a wish."

We plan our weddings, vacations and home renovations.

We do not plan our lives with our children. We don't lay out the life skills our children need to learn and then create a plan to achieve what we desire.

We are winging it with the ones we love most in the world, our babies. We demand respect. We dictate and control every aspect of their lives and then wonder what's wrong with them.

Thomas and I know that right now you are reacting to and cleaning up after your kids most of every day in a chaotic, exhausting and frustrating environment. Right?

To learn anything we must first see what it actually should look like. Then, we need a good learning environment so we can experience it on our own. This is the only way. We must experience the difference so we can make a choice and engage in free will.

Seeing creates awareness. Doing over and over again creates life skill. Let's say you want your children to put their toys away. Yelling at them, "Put your toys away" is a dictation and is a habit that is not serving you.

You must show your child what it looks like, mess it all back up, and then have them show you what it looks like.

Look, the truth is that you've been domesticated, trained and conditioned to believe that to be a good parent means to do everything for your children. Thank you, Dr. Spock.

In today's society, if you have your child make their own lunch, someone is going to call you a bad parent.

Well, so what? Who cares what they think?

If you don't teach your child how to feed themselves now, how are they ever going to survive if something happens to you?

If you don't teach your child that they're good enough to make lunch on their own, how are they ever going to believe they can live a full life without you?

If you want order, peace and laughter, doesn't it make sense that you should do the opposite of the perfect scientific equation for bad feelings?

Let's take a look at what creates more love and joy...

Parent's Plan + Child's Practiced Action = Harmonious Effect.

This means that if you have a goal and your child has a goal, all you have to do is proactively develop a plan that both of you can focus working on.

Your job is to create a plan for your child to follow, and then to teach your child the matching life skills.

Have you ever played Simon Says? That's a wonderful example of a game you can play with your child that will teach self-control, focus and following directions.

Your child's job is to engage in learning said life skills by following what you teach them. Can you see how important it is to develop a plan and give proactive attention to your children?

When you have a family plan in place, there'll be no questions like "What do I do when my child does this?"

If little Timmy decides to have a temper tantrum, your proactive plan for what happens next should be crystal clear for both you and your child — before anger sets in.

"When little Timmy chooses to have a temper tantrum, little Timmy is choosing to go hang out in his room for a few minutes." It's not punishment. It's proactive and agreed upon plan based on the actions your child chooses.

When you decide everything in advance, your child's entire learning environment will transform from reactive to proactive.

You'll have a vision.

You'll be more confident and so will your child.

Think about it like this...when your child is upset about something, they're basically coming to you as a customer service department. You're the person in charge.

They don't have the skills or vocabulary to tell you "Hey, Mom! I need life skills here."

They're telling you in the only way they know how. They throw temper tantrums. They seem depressed or angry. They whine. They cry. They hit.

Because of constant dictation and control, your children are just figuring things out on their own. Since whining has worked for them in the past, they'll continue to escalate the same known life skill throughout childhood. If not already evaluated, this pattern will lead to that child eventually becoming labeled with a behavior or emotional disorder and prescribed medication.

Think about this for a moment...if you went to a customer service department to complain because a product you bought didn't work and you didn't know how to fix it, how would you like them to respond?

What if they responded with "I'm sorry, I don't do that"?

Wouldn't you be angry?

"Listen, you are not hearing me! Obviously you're deaf, so I'm going to yell louder."

Maybe your child has never learned the simple game of opposites. They won't know they can turn obstacles into opportunities unless you teach them that. Maybe your child has never learned to negotiate or been shown what respect looks like.

Demanding your child respect you does not show them what it looks like.

If you change the root cause, you must change the effect, yes?

Choose what life skills your children need to learn and then teach them until they can duplicate your efforts!

Action Plan: Begin at once to create a master list of life skills you still need to teach your child before he or she becomes an adult. As soon as your list is in writing, it becomes a goal.

Turn That Frown Upside Down

Children love showing off their greatness. You know this by how often your child shouts, "Look what I did, Mom!" More opportunity to be independent is the cure for the lack of confidence we see in today's children. After all, if a parent does for the child what they should be doing on their own, the message is clear. "You don't think I have what it takes to do it on my own."

It's okay if they fail.

Allow your children to fail.

Encouraging your child to persevere through obstacles will help them develop neural pathways that will set them up for a massive amount of success later in life — no matter what they do.

Validation is empowering. Recognizing what's important to your child is going to pay off huge dividends both now and later on in life!

Validating everything they ask for will bring you and your child more confidence and feelings of worthiness.

You only know what you know. What you know has been passed down to you unconsciously from people who loved you the most, your parents.

What end result are you looking for? Isn't it more empowerment and love than what you remember as a child?

I once heard a story of a woman who brought home a ham for Christmas dinner. Before she placed it in the pot to cook it, she cut both ends off the ham. Her daughter was watching and asked, "Mom, why do you cut the ends off the ham?"

Mom paused a moment and then answered, "I don't really know. That's just what I've always done. I saw my Mom doing that when I was a little girl."

When Grandma arrived for Christmas dinner, the question was brought up: "Grandma, why did you cut the ends off the ham before placing it in the oven?"

"I don't really know," Grandma replied. "Your great-grandma used to do that, so it's just something I've always done!"

Later, the family all traveled to Great-Grandma's house to share Christmas tea. During a lull in the conversation, the granddaughter asked, "Nana, why do you cut the ends off the ham before cooking it?"

"Well," replied the great-grandmother, "when your grandma was a girl, my oven was very small and I couldn't fit the whole ham in without cutting the ends off."

Now, I don't know if this is a real story or not, but why would we continue to do what we already know doesn't work just because that's what our parents did? It's because that's all we know to do unless we begin to educate ourselves on purpose!

It's time to think for ourselves and to step up for the sake of our children. Don't you think?

Taking the time to acknowledge what your child is interested in versus automatically telling them no is life-changing in itself.

Do you want to follow the equation that will guarantee you joy-filled days of laughter with your kids? All you need to do is make a plan to achieve your desire and attach them to your child's desires.

(Parent Goal + Child Goal) + Parent Plan + Child Action = Desired Effect.

Here's how it works:

You have a goal called healthy, happy, cooperative kids.

Your child has a goal for a cookie.

You validate what's important to him.

- Share your parent-approved plan with your child.

Teach them to do exactly what you want through role play.

Give them something to work for!

I'm sure you can see how this will create a win-win plan versus a win-lose plan. You know, where you win and they lose? "Why won't they just listen to me?" And, you kind of lose too, don't you?

You: "I'd love for you to have a cookie. Did you want half a cookie, a whole cookie or two cookies?"

Your child: "Ummm…I want two cookies."

You: "Perfect! When you sit at the table like this…" And then show him what that looks like before you get him to copy you, showing you what it looks like. "…And you eat some of your dinner, you'll make half a cookie show up. If you eat all your dinner but get up from the dinner table, you can make one cookie show up. But, if you sit at the table like this and you eat all your dinner, you can make two cookies show up."

Perfecting the skill of pre-framing looks easy but takes a little or, in some cases, a lot of practice. Most of us have been dictating and punishing for a number of years already. Those parenting skills are deeply ingrained and habitual.

At first, making the change from hellish to heavenly will feel like it did when you learned to tie your shoes or drive a car. It's going to feel uncomfortable. It will be worth it!

Consciously learning to become a proactive parent will mean you get to be your child's superhero. You can instill all of the life skills and characteristics you choose for them to know in a loving and guiding way!

You won't have to be the bearer of bad news. You won't have to be your child's opponent by telling him no. You won't need to yell at your child ever again. Ever!

You'll know exactly how to inspire your children to work towards the goals they choose for themselves.

A child builds confidence by persevering through struggle while working towards things that are important to them until they succeed.

Let's say your child asks for a $500 bike. They don't understand money yet. Even teenagers don't know money. They have never had to earn it. Let's say that this child is between the ages of eight and 12.

They don't understand you have to put in 14 hours of overtime to earn enough money for a down payment. There is no way for them to understand that concept.

"Hi, Mom! I'm so excited! I saw this bike. It's so cool. All the cool kids have one."

You would probably go into rescue mode and feel responsible. Right? What if you really can't afford it?

"Yeah, sorry. We can't afford that right now." Can you see the look of devastation in your child's face? What feeling matches that outcome? Is it a good or bad feeling?

They hear "no" to what's important to them. They feel unworthy. They feel hopeless. If you can't make it happen there must be no way to make it happen. You're his superhero!

A Short message from Mommy's Angels:

Hey, are you enjoying the book? I'd love to hear your thoughts!

Many readers do not know how hard reviews are to come by, and how much they help an author.

I would be incredibly thankful if you could take just 60 seconds to write a brief review on Amazon, even if it's just a few sentences!

>> Click here to leave a quick review

Thank you for taking the time to share your thoughts!

Your review will genuinely make a difference for me and help gain exposure for my work.

Chapter 5 Discipline and Your Toddler

No doubt, you would like to have a well-behaved child. You may even be feeling pressure from family members, friends, and strangers you meet on the street to make sure your mini-me stays polite and quiet. Here's the good news: You can have a well-behaved child. The bad news: You can't have one all of the time. By the very nature of human brain development, our children require time, patience, and guidance to learn how to treat others with respect and regulate their own emotional states.

What Is Discipline?

How do you make a child behave? The answer may be shocking: you don't. The child alone is able to choose to modify their behavior within the scope of their current developmental capabilities. But you have a lot of power as the child's parent. You can help them make the choice to comply or cooperate with your requests, and you can teach them about the behavioral expectations for different situations in your culture. Your child needs discipline. To use the transitive verb to bring home the point, your child needs to be disciplined by you.

A better approach to disciplining your child is to use techniques that foster their ability to make moral judgments about right and wrong for themselves. This does not mean letting the child do whatever they want. While they are a toddler, you are the one responsible for making any major decisions that you feel are in their best interest. Since a toddler lacks the cognitive ability to use reason or logic to solve problems or decide what behavior is appropriate in any given situation, you will be coaching them step-by-step. Their budding independence will emerge by making simple, meaningful choices at first. When your child releases their big emotions and loses control, you will offer your support by empathizing and giving them the boundaries they need in order to feel safe and loved.

Setting Realistic Goals

Parents often have expectations for behavior that aren't realistic given the ages of their children. This will help you know whether the technique you are choosing will support your short- or long-term goals for your child's growth and development.

Short-Term Goals

There will be times when you need to set a limit and either commit to enforcing it quickly or let go of your ideal routine. Here are few examples of some common short-term goals related to behavioral issues.

•Compliance for the sake of safety: see Distract and Redirect

•Getting a good night's sleep: see Bedtime Struggles

•Using good manners: see Going Out in Public

•Stopping the whining: see Putting an End to the Whining

Disciplining your often unreasonable, highly emotional toddler can be frustrating. To remind yourself of these long-term goals, you might even keep this list in a place where you will see it daily, such as on the refrigerator, in your purse, or by the front door.

Temperament and Behavior

Your parenting style will have a significant influence on how your child behaves and perceives their place in the world, but it is not the only factor by far. Many people assume that a child's personality is always the direct result of how permissive or dictatorial the parent is. This is a myth. Your child is a unique and valuable person, born with a predisposition toward certain traits that developed in utero and continued to be formed by their experiences throughout early childhood.

In a revolutionary 1970 study of infant reactions to stimuli, Alexander Thomas, Stella Chess, and Herbert G. Birch determined that a child's "personality is formed by the constant interplay of temperament and environment." The nine temperament traits identified in this study give us insight into why children raised in similar environments may behave differently from one another.

Activity level: This trait refers to your child's general energy level. A high-energy child can be a handful with all the squirming and wiggling, while a more sedentary child can be hard to motivate physically, as quiet, calm activities are preferred. If your toddler is constantly climbing the furniture, running in circles, and popping in and out of bed at night, provide ample access to the outdoors on a daily basis so that her muscles have the freedom to move. Indoors, focus on ways to safely meet your child's need to stretch and explore independently.

Rhythmicity: How predictable is your child's natural, biological rhythm? Some children will eat, sleep, and have bowel movements with extreme regularity. For them, a predictable schedule is a comfortable one and largely self-determined. Other children show much more irregularity, which can complicate meals, naps, and toilet learning. Parental intervention and flexibility are necessary to avoid conflict.

Distractibility: Is your child easily distracted by outside influences? A child with high distractibility will often be satisfied when you exchange an unsafe object for a safe toy or when you sing a song while performing an unappealing task, such as buckling a car seat or changing a diaper. A child who is less willing to be distracted will not stop fussing until the task has been completed.

Initial response: When confronted with a new situation, such as a new person, food, toy, or activity, how eagerly does your child embrace the new experience? Some children approach them with ease, immediately interacting and engaging impulsively. Others are slow to warm up, taking time to get comfortable and assess the situation. When you introduce your child to a new person, such as a babysitter, the child may prefer to sit quietly in your lap observing for a while before interacting. However, the withdrawal of some children from new experiences is much more dramatic and requires considerable adult encouragement and patience. A child with a negative initial response to new situations will cry, hide, or run away. They will need emotional support and lots of time to adjust to new experiences.

Adaptability: This refers to your child's ability to adjust over time to new experiences, routines, or expectations. If your child is adaptable in temperament, transitioning from one activity to another will not be a big deal. Settling into a new schedule may take some time, but you will not typically encounter much resistance from your child. Other children will react adversely to new routines, as evidenced by tantrums, defiance, or anxious behaviors. These children will benefit from more gradual shifts in routine rather than dramatic ones.

Attention span and persistence: Does your child concentrate on a single activity for a long time? Do they continue to repeat and practice new skills despite any obstacles in their way? The child with higher levels of attention and persistence will not give up easily when asked to perform tasks that are initially frustrating. On the other hand, if you interrupt this same child to ask them to move on to another activity, you may be met with resistance and an inflexible attitude. If your child has a shorter attention span and less persistence, they may need a more step-by-step approach, reminders, and visual cues to help them complete difficult tasks.

The intensity of reaction: How strongly does your child show their emotions? Very intense children may be labeled as "overdramatic," celebrating with extreme exuberance when excited and sobbing or throwing tantrums over minor disappointments. Children with lower levels of intensity may smile or cry, but in general their reaction to events will be much more subdued by comparison.

Sensory threshold: In response to varied physical sensations, does your child react positively, negatively, or not at all? Some children are sensitive and easily overwhelmed by sensory input, such as noise, light, or textures, which makes crowded, noisy places difficult to navigate. Others will react in the opposite way and will seek out more stimulation on purpose.

Quality of mood: Does your child tend to be cheerful and upbeat or have a distrustful and serious demeanor? Your child's moods will of course vary from day to day, but in general, most children lean toward a more positive emotional state or a more negative one.

Human personalities are uniquely different, but all are beautiful and complementary. No matter where a child falls on the spectrum of each of these temperamental traits, they deserve to be understood and valued for who they are and who they are becoming. Certain situations will be easier for your child to deal with, and some discipline strategies will work better for them than others. By understanding the way they approach life's experiences, you will be able to empathize with your child's struggles, choose the most effective parenting techniques, and lovingly guide their toward adulthood.

Parent to Parent: Loving Those Personality Differences

"My 3-year-old is very sensitive. He needs time to adjust to new situations and warm up to people, although he craves physical affection with us. He is also very caring, independent, logical, and clever. He is an outside-of-the-box thinker. I definitely need to empathize with him a lot and give him space and time he needs to get used to a new place or new people. Everyone calls him shy, but he is just cautious. He also gets very frustrated pretty easily. He needs someone to be gentle with him and not dismiss his worries.

"I knew from the beginning that my second child was his opposite. My younger daughter is laid back and goes with the flow. She can handle a lot of things my son could not as an infant, such as missed or delayed naps, and she is more independent. I strive to follow peaceful and gentle parenting practices with both."

— Kate, 32, from Crown Point,
 Indiana, parent of two children
 (ages 3 years and 10 months)

Age-Appropriate Discipline

Your child's general temperament may stay fairly constant from infancy, but the natural course of human development is not a steady path. As your child grows older, their needs, interests, and behaviors will shift, sometimes dramatically, and therefore your discipline strategies must also cater to their present self, not to the child they were before.

Using the "distract and redirect" technique is often very effective and easy to implement for a 1-year-old, even if your child's temperament is fairly low in distractibility.

However, a few years later, this same technique is not likely to go over well, as 4-year-olds have longer attention spans and a clearer understanding of how to follow rules. At age 3 and above, most children are able to make the connection between their actions and the natural consequences, but not before. Sparking the imagination is a technique that speaks especially to a 4-year-old's proclivity for pretend play, while a 1-year-old would just be confused.

In this book, you will find suggestions for techniques that generally work well for children at specific ages, given their current developmental capabilities.

Choose Your Approach

If I had to honestly describe my general approach to disciplining my own children, it would be fairly well encapsulated in these three words: patient, empathetic, and silly. As a highly emotional optimist, I often start the mornings with my young children by singing a familiar upbeat song, followed by raspberry-belly-induced giggling, and then a gentle reminder about the day's upcoming activities.

If one of my children begins to act out, I typically watch and wait first to see if my child will change his behavior on his own before I intervene, and I'm gifted at conveying my empathy. However, I do struggle with organization and routines. My spontaneous, impulsive personality can conflict with my children's need for structure. I may personally lean toward being a bit too messy and goofy, but I strongly identify with other parents who use a gentle or positive approach to discipline.

Now it's your turn to craft your own approach to discipline. Your personality and outlook on life will greatly influence how you communicate with your child. Do you tend to be quieter or more boisterous? Do you enjoy flexibility or are you more rigid by nature? What is your tolerance for frustration? Do you typically see the glass as half-full or half-empty? Your child's temperament and age will also influence what disciplinary techniques are most effective. Finally, think about the long-term goals you consider most important to help your child learn right now. With these personal preferences in mind and the wide variety of techniques explained throughout this book, you will be on your way to creating a consistent philosophy of your own.

How to Use This Book

This book has been designed as a practical guide to understanding and managing your toddler's behavior. To help you navigate the transitions both into and out of toddlerhood, I have included information for a 4-year age span.

•An overview of your child's physical, cognitive, and social-emotional development

•Effective and age-appropriate discipline techniques

•Common behavioral issues with suggested strategies for overcoming them

Throughout the book, you will find sidebars and boxes with tips for navigating tricky situations, reminders of how to best communicate with your child, and advice from parents who have been in similar situations.

Keep in mind that child development is not a linear process. Your child may reach milestones sooner or later than another child who is the same age. The developmental notes are generalizations for each age group.

The suggested disciplinary techniques in this book do build upon one another from year to year. This flexibility will allow you to curate your own approach to discipline based on the needs of your child.

Specific behaviors also vary greatly depending on your child's temperament and other environmental factors. For example, tantrums may simply not be an issue for you until your child is past the age of 2, whereas another child may have severe tantrums as a 1-year-old and none by age 3. When a topic is not covered in one age group, it's perfectly fine to skip around either before or after your child's biological age to find strategies for specific behavioral issues.

In-Depth Look: Be Your Own Sounding Board

Getting to the root of a challenging behavioral situation and deciding how to handle it requires objectivity— something of which all parents are in perpetual short supply! If you have a friend or willing partner to listen, that is a fantastic way to gain clarity. If not, you can be your own sounding board. Start by asking and answering these three big questions:

1. Can I allow my child's current behavior to continue? Only you can decide if the answer to this question is yes or no, but before you use any disciplinary technique, you

need to know why you are choosing to allow the behavior or why you must stop it. There is so much to be said for letting things go unless you are fully ready and willing to follow through. Many of the challenging behaviors we see in our children have developmental reasons or are a sign of your child's temperament. If the activity in question is a reasonable one for the age of your child and isn't doing any real harm to anyone or anything, consider letting it go or changing the situation slightly so that you can allow it.

2. Am I allowing for independence and providing security? Many conflicts between adults and children occur because of the tension between the child's natural desire to acquire new skills, as modeled by the adults around them, and the desire for adult supervision and protection that will keep them safe as they explore. Effective parenting is never prescriptive. Like a scientist, before you come to a solution, you must observe, experiment, analyze, and then make changes if necessary.

3. Am I focused on building a relationship based on trust and respect? Take a close look at how you are responding to your child's behavior. Are you committed to nurturing a healthy relationship between the two of

you? Disciplinary strategies that are belittling, threatening, manipulative, deceiving, coercive, or sarcastic may gain your child's obedience, but they will not gain your child's cooperation. Trust is earned, not demanded.

What you are aiming for is authentic, gentle loving guidance with clear limits. Answering these three questions will get you closer to that ideal.

Chapter 6 Managing Difficult Emotions

Facing Discomfort

Picture this: It's a beautiful summer morning, and you're taking the kids to the beach for the day. You've gotten up early to pack sunblock and towels. The kids are still asleep, and all is quiet in the house, but instead of feeling excited about the outing, you find yourself feeling anxious, tense, and even frustrated. Thoughts of your defiant child starting arguments in the car or having a meltdown over the smallest request flash through your mind. You remember the last time you attempted a family trip to the beach and had to turn around before you got there because your child had a violent tantrum. Your anxiety and frustration then turn to guilt, maybe even shame. You tell yourself that today may be different. Still, you can't shake your negative mood, and your worries persist. Does this sound familiar? This is the reality for most families living with ODD.

Your brain has been programmed through repeated experiences with your ODD child to anticipate the worst. You're not feeling on edge around your kid because you want to—your brain is just trying to keep you safe by anticipating problems. Your child's prickly behavior has likely become a huge wedge in your relationship. Parents I work with often report painful, conflicted feelings about their ODD child. Facing the discomfort of these difficult feelings, and learning how to act calmly even when you're feeling them, is an important part of making progress.

Anger, Sadness, Fear, and Shame

You might feel the urge to skip past this section. Who wants to dwell on anger, sadness, fear, or shame? But understanding how these emotions impact you and your relationships is crucial.

First, I want to emphasize that all your negative feelings are totally normal. They're valid reactions to the situation you're in, and it's okay to feel them. I'd also encourage you to take a closer look at some of your most potent emotions, like anger, and see what else is lurking within them. As it turns out, sadness is often the driving force behind anger and guilt; we often prefer to avoid the vulnerability of sadness by covering it over with a secondary emotion. As unpleasant as anger may be, it feels more powerful to be mad than to be sad—but the sense of control it provides rarely lasts. I'm willing to bet that a lot of your anger at your ODD child stems from sadness for your child's struggle and fear for their future.

Parents also report feeling guilt and shame when talking about their feelings toward their defiant child. Both emotions are understandable, but guilt, though painful, is far more useful than shame. In proper doses, guilt allows you to see how you may have inadvertently contributed to your child's behavior problems. If correctly channeled, it can lead to problem-solving and to changing your own behavior. Shame, on the other hand, is usually toxic. Shame will tell you you're a bad parent and the reason your child is acting out. Rather than motivating you the way guilt can, shame often keeps parents from seeking the help they need.

We've established that parenting an ODD child means you're dealing with a lot of strong, unpleasant emotions. We also know, because you're reading this book, that you're determined to make progress with your child despite the pain or anxiety you're feeling. One helpful step toward progress lies in changing not how we feel but rather our relationship to our most difficult feelings. Strategies including mindfulness, acceptance and commitment therapy (ACT), and cognitive behavioral therapy (CBT) are especially useful here. Mindfulness practices can be particularly helpful in creating some distance between us and our strongest emotions. Opening a small gap between having the initial feeling— say, anger—and acting on it can help us keep our cool even in difficult situations.

MEDITATION: Observing Your Emotions and Thoughts

Set aside five minutes in a quiet, comfortable place. Set a timer or your phone alarm.

Take one minute and focus entirely on deep breathing. Breathe in deeply through your nose, and slowly release through your mouth. Your in breaths should be so deep that it feels like your abdomen is expanding, only to be reduced on your out breaths. When you notice your attention wandering, refocus on your breathing.

Close your eyes, and for two minutes focus entirely on what emotions you're experiencing. Let your body give you clues, if needed. If you can't pinpoint the feeling(s), just notice if you're comfortable or uncomfortable.

Now, imagine a beautiful blue sky with puffy white clouds and a gentle breeze blowing them past. Picture yourself carefully placing each emotion you're feeling onto the passing clouds.

Notice how the clouds float past you with the breeze. First they were right in front of you, and now they're gone in the distance. If some clouds stay for a while, let them be. The wind will ease them away soon.

If you find yourself judging the feeling or becoming distracted, focus on the fluffy clouds and the gentle breeze.

Next, do the same with your thoughts for two minutes.

Place all the words and sentences running through your mind onto the clouds. No matter how distracting or distressing, let the thought clouds float past. Remember, they're just thoughts and have no power in themselves. You can notice what they look and feel like without doing anything about them. You can just let them float past.

If they become stuck, or you begin to judge them, that's normal. Just let them be until they're ready to float past.

When the timer sounds, take five deep breaths to end the meditation.

The Avoidance Trap

Avoidance—the attempt to dodge and/or suppress painful feelings, thoughts, and situations—is enticing. It's a natural human response to pain and distress, and it promises comfort in the face of discomfort. Unfortunately, the more we avoid the things that trigger difficult emotions, the more overwhelming those things become, which only motivates us to avoid them more. And when your child is the source of your discomfort, avoidance can greatly undermine your parenting and your child's potential for growth and change. The goal of healthy coping is not to push away the inevitable difficulties that arise in life but to tolerate and accept them—and move forward despite their presence.

Avoidance can show up in all sorts of ways and isn't always as obvious as physically avoiding whatever's distressing you (by, for example, sending your defiant child to their room when things get heated). Here are some common ways I've seen avoidance play out in the families of ODD kids.

Resignation/despair: By the time families come to my office, they're often highly discouraged. Parents will report, "There's no hope," "Nothing works," or, "I cannot do any more than I'm already doing." Clinging to resignation may help you avoid fear and sadness, but it offers no hope for change.

Placating/giving in: Tired of big meltdowns? I don't blame you. Unfortunately, giving in to your defiant child in an attempt to avoid blowouts only reinforces their unruly behaviors. Commonly, this form of avoidance manifests itself in inconsistency—e.g., not following through with stated consequences or inadvertently rewarding inappropriate behaviors to keep the peace.

Excessive control/punishment: Some parents try to avoid the discomfort of their child's behavior by inflicting punishment and control. Their intention is usually to help the child behave appropriately through strict rules, with harsh punishments to enforce compliance. While structure is necessary for ODD kids, this avoidance strategy often backfires because it prevents the child from feeling capable of succeeding and creates unnecessary friction.

Justification/blame: Another common avoidance strategy is making excuses or blaming others for a defiant child's behavior ("she was too tired," "the teacher was really hard on him"). Emotionally, this allows the parent to avoid seeing the child as "bad," but it also splits the child into "good" and "bad" parts when they're really a whole being with complex needs.

Separation/disconnecting: Psychologically, it's challenging to be emotionally connected to an ODD kid who is simultaneously lovable and frightening. Parents might try to avoid that challenge by separating themselves emotionally from their child. I often hear parents say, "I just can't connect with him," "I love her, but I don't like her," or, "I don't feel the same about him as I do my other children." These parents love their children very much, but they're also overwhelmed, and sometimes they build avoidant psychological defenses against that.

Anger: Parents who live with the daily struggle of caring for a defiant child often develop a thick skin of anger to avoid feelings of sadness and fear. The developmental trajectory of a defiant child is frightening and painful, especially without intervention. Because anger allows us to feel less vulnerable than fear and pain, it can seem like a welcome relief. Unfortunately, it does little to actually solve the problems ODD presents.

Though these avoidance strategies may offer short-term comfort, in the long run they only cause more distress by perpetuating unhealthy behavior patterns instead of facing them head-on and solving them.

Getting Unstuck

Now that we've reviewed the most common avoidance traps, it's time to start learning how to get out of them. Getting unstuck means, first of all, acknowledging that you're currently stuck. Since you're reading this book, you probably recognize you need some help shaking loose from the unhelpful behavior patterns you're caught in with your child.

Of the avoidance traps described above, which ones best describe your situation? Now is the time to take an honest look at how your actions are contributing to your child's defiance. I say that not to place blame or shame but rather to provide a starting place for transformation. Since we can change only the things we acknowledge, I encourage you to be as candid as possible when it comes to identifying your stuck points. Do you find yourself disconnecting from your child when overwhelmed? Is giving in to their tantrums easier than holding your ground? Does your anger get out of control, leaving you feeling ashamed and guilty?

Recognizing these things is hard—but not as hard as remaining stuck. You have more power to change this situation than you think.

WRITTEN EXERCISE: A Letter to Your Child

The following exercise is intended to help you express your feelings toward your child in an open, honest, and safe way. You will not give the letter to your child; rather it's an opportunity for you to acknowledge the impact that your child's behavior has had on you and the hopes and dreams you still have for them.

In your notebook, write a letter to your child, which will not be delivered, by answering the following prompts:

•When you were born, these were my hopes and dreams for you.

•This is what I love about you. (List qualities you admire and reasons you love your child.)

•These are my hopes for you in the future. (What do you want most for them?)

•This is how your words, actions, and attitude have made me feel about myself and about you. (Be as honest as possible, even though it may be very painful.)

•This is the impact that your behavior and ODD symptoms have had on my life. (Include the influence on your other relationships, career, well-being, beliefs, and goals.)

•These are the ways I've tried to cope. (Note helpful and unhelpful coping skills you've tried.)

•These are the uncomfortable thoughts, feelings, and situations I've tried to avoid in order to manage the impact of your actions on me. (List avoidance strategies used.)

•This is why I still feel hopeful. (If you're reading this, then there's at least a bit of hope—what is it?)

Once you've written the letter, you may wish to shred it or put it away somewhere safe. The purpose of the letter is to express your pain and acknowledge the impact ODD has had on you so you can move forward to the next phase of this work.

The Power of Acceptance

We've talked a lot about avoidance and why we tend to run away from difficult thoughts, feelings, and situations. If you're like most people, you might be asking yourself what you're supposed to do with the discomfort you're feeling. After all, if you can't avoid it, then you're just stuck with it, right? Wrong. The key is acceptance. In psychological terms, acceptance means allowing yourself to experience thoughts, emotions, or situations without trying to change them or push them away.

I liken the acceptance process to a game of tug-of-war where you're on one end of the rope and the painful feeling, thought, or experience is on the other. The more you pull, the harder your opponent pulls in response. Psychologically, this means that the more effort you put into resisting the experience, the greater the intensity, duration, and frequency of that experience in your life. In this metaphor, acceptance means letting go of the rope. When you do that, the fight between you and the distressing situation ceases, because you're no longer participating in the battle.

Properly practiced, acceptance helps you grow more comfortable with your discomfort. I know that sounds paradoxical, but it works. Bottling up negative thoughts and feelings can lead to depression, anxiety, health problems, and unhelpful coping strategies, which only fuel your distress. Acceptance is the best, most realistic way to meet your emotional challenges in a healthy way.

Life is full of distressing events, from small disappointments to heartbreaking losses. Since there's no way to avoid them, the best way through is to accept their presence as part of life—and learn to move forward anyway.

I want to take a moment to differentiate between acceptance and giving up. In ACT, acceptance is not about giving up; rather, it's a highly active and intentional process. Acceptance is far harder to do than the passive process of resigning yourself to negative thoughts, feelings, and experiences, because it requires persistence and a commitment to your values and aspirations.

MEDITATION: Inviting Difficult Emotions

This meditation will help you work on your ability to tolerate distressing feelings. It's a safe, structured way to practice becoming comfortable with discomfort.

At the end of the day, set aside 10 minutes in a quiet, comfortable place. Set an alarm if you wish.

Take one minute and focus entirely on deep breathing. Breathe in deeply through your nose, and slowly release through your mouth. Your in breathing should be deep enough that you feel your abdomen expanding when you inhale.

If you notice your attention wandering, refocus on your breathing.

Close your eyes and consider all the things that happened to you today from the time you woke up until this very moment. Let all the highs and lows pass through your consciousness.

Now, think of the hardest part of your day. Notice the thoughts and feelings that arise as you recall this difficult experience. Are they comfortable or uncomfortable? If you notice yourself resisting any thoughts or feelings, try to just sit with them as they are.

Notice your body as you remember this hard point in your day. From the top of your head down to your toes, recognize any sensations you may be experiencing, including warmth, tension, or pain. Allow these feelings to be.

Take five deep breaths in through your nose, slowly exhaling through your mouth.

Imagine yourself gently picking up the difficult feelings from today's challenging experience. Imagine them in the palm of your hand. Notice how they look and feel, the weight of them. See them from all angles.

If you notice you're becoming distracted, just return your attention to the feelings. When you're done, imagine placing the feelings gently beside you.

It is now time to get a better look at your thoughts about today's difficulty. Imagine them as a slow stream of words flowing past you like the breeze. See each letter; note the size and color of the font. See them as they are: a collection of words strung together. Let them swirl around you until they're just letters.

Take five deep breaths and envision all of your painful, difficult thoughts, feelings, and physical sensations before you. Really see them in full detail. Let them know that they are valid.

Now, visualize yourself in the midst of this discomfort and remind yourself that you are strong enough to hold these hard things.

Take five last deep breaths and slowly open your eyes. How do you feel? What are you noticing?

Turning toward Pain

How do we learn to accept distress when our brains are programmed to avoid painful things? The first step is to practice turning toward the pain we would normally try to suppress or work around. Every day you experience a whole range of emotions, whether you're aware of them all or not. You may feel irritated in traffic, then anxious about a big conference call, then excited about dinner plans. Feelings, and the thoughts that accompany them, come and go constantly.

It's human nature to push away what's negative, but while this might offer you short-term relief, it's not a remedy for pain. Instead, it exacerbates it. But when you consciously choose to lean in to your painful feelings, you're focusing on what's happening in the present moment instead of resisting reality.

Are you willing to learn to accept the pain as a means of moving past it? ACT focuses on living in line with your values and being committed to actions that support those values, no matter how you're feeling from moment to moment. For you, this may look like being open to the pain of seeing your child struggle while still being engaged with them because you value your relationship. It could also allow for you to have more self-acceptance rather than self-criticism and doubt. Turning toward discomfort is initially very challenging, but it becomes easier with practice.

Moving Forward Despite Challenges

In working toward long-term, sustainable changes for you and your child, you're taking on a huge challenge. The journey won't always be smooth. You'll stumble and perhaps at times fall. If that happens, remember: This work is hard because it matters—a lot. Helping your child make gains requires new skills, for them and for you. It also requires changes on your part that may seem counterintuitive or uncomfortably different from your usual MO. Be gentle with yourself as you go through this process. The goal is not perfection but persistence. Bumps in the road give you information about what areas need more time or work. There's no need to rush. The more time you allow for new habits to form, the greater the likelihood that you'll carry them into the future.

<u>WRITTEN EXERCISE</u>: <u>Acceptance</u>

"Why does my son get so angry?" "Why can't I get through to my daughter?" "Why is life so hard!?" Asking "why" questions can keep us stuck, because they focus our attention on how we think things ought to be rather than on reality.

In your notebook, make a list of 10 "why" questions that you often ask about yourself, your child, or challenging situations. Then go back and rewrite them, changing them from questions into statements. For example, "Why can't I get through to her?" could be revised to, "I can't get through to her." "Why is life so hard?" might become, "Life is so hard." The goal is to help you refocus your thoughts on the present and see and accept things as they are in the moment, rather than judging them.

- Action Plan: Self-Care

Self-care is an essential element of well-being. Taking care of yourself isn't selfish—it's a prerequisite for caring for others. I like to think of self-care as a discipline, something to be practiced, like dance or painting. If you're like most parents I work with, you're probably thinking, I don't have time for that. I get it. You're incredibly busy and stressed by life's demands. But taking time to nurture yourself is essential. You can't get water from a dry well; self-care is how you fill yourself back up.

Create a self-care plan for the next seven days. Think for a minute about things that nourish or soothe you. They don't need to be elaborate activities. They should be simple enough that you'll actually do them.

In your notebook or planner, schedule one self-care activity each day. It's important to write your intentions down, because we tend to commit more to a task that we've set down in writing. Here are some suggestions to get you started. Don't be afraid to mix it up!

Meditations or guided imagery: Research shows the effectiveness of mediations and guided imagery as a means of increasing positive mood. There are countless meditation scripts available on Pinterest and YouTube. Keep these to 10 minutes or less.

Mindfulness: This is the practice of being aware of the present moment. A popular mindfulness activity: Take two minutes to notice five things you see, four things you hear, three things you can touch, two things you can smell, and one thing you can taste. This helps ground you in the present moment.

Exercise: Exercise is important for your physical and mental health. It releases endorphins that help improve mood, relieve stress, and reduce mild depression and anxiety symptoms. You don't need to exercise super hard or long; a 15-minute walk or stretch session will do.

Gratitude: Practicing gratitude has been shown to increase positive emotion. Try listing three things you're thankful for each day, or make a "gratitude jar" where you can drop in a daily note of gratitude for something or someone.

Quality time: Spending time with those you care about—or even a family pet—is a great way to refill your well. Just be sure that you're present, not tuning out by staring at your phone or the television.

Takeaways

•Facing uncomfortable feelings and thoughts is a necessary part of this work.

•Anger, sadness, anxiety, guilt, and shame are common, natural feelings for parents struggling to help their child with ODD.

•Avoidance of painful feelings, thoughts, and situations only makes them worse.

•Acceptance is the practice of allowing room for distressing emotions and thoughts without trying to change or get rid of them.

•Acceptance is an active process.

•Self-care is necessary, not selfish. You can't give back to others if you have nothing left in your own well.

•Self-care is a discipline that takes time and practice to become consistent.

Chapter 7 Make Requests Rather Than Demands

Adults often think it is the job of children to comply or follow directions. When children do not do as directed, they are often labeled as noncompliant. There is a great deal of professional literature on teaching compliance to children. Stickers, stars, or tokens are often a part of this goal. Furthermore, these external reinforcers may even interfere with the child's natural desire to do what is being asked. But is there any alternative to compliance, when it comes to children's behavior?

Conventional advice is for adults to make clear commands to children. However, such commands can sometimes contribute to a child's defiance. In addition, when adults make commands, it tends to lead to similar power displays in children's behavior. Commanding is very similar to demanding, and we usually want children to give up their own demandingness. Yet conventional advice preaches that we tell children to do what we say, rather than what we do.

We often command children to do things that are in their best interests, instead of helping them see the value behind the request. In contrast, we can work with the child to put both the adult's needs and the child's needs on the table. This helps children learn that everyone's needs matter equally. Consequently, they receive a valuable model of cooperation.

When an adult tells a child to do something, without being open to the child's reaction, the child is likely to experience some resistance. For some children, this resistance may be demonstrated in a variety of behavior issues. Children want to participate in making the decisions that affect them. Instead of compliance, a more useful goal may be cooperation.

We can often make use of children's natural tendency to cooperate by asking them (rather than demanding) for something that we would like. Some children may cooperate simply due to an inherent desire to connect with others. If the child sees the value behind the request, the likelihood of cooperation increases further.

We can make requests using the same respectful approach an adult would use when asking a respected person for something. There is a prevalent notion that it is children's responsibility to comply with adults. However, there is value in choice, and we ultimately want children to act based on the inherent value of their actions.

From the perspective of NVC, a request has several elements. First of all, we ask the person to do something rather than NOT to do something. Framing the request in this way also makes it easier for children to know what is being asked of them. Second, requests involve asking for something that the child is able to do. If the request is beyond the child's cognitive or physical capacity, then we are likely to be met with a negative response. A third element of a request is to ask for concrete actions that the child can do in the moment. Putting together just the first three elements, we would ask Jill to take her sibling to a movie, rather than asking her to stop bothering the sibling. A fourth element of a request is that we are willing to hear "no" as an answer. If we get angry when the request is not met with a "yes," we have really made a demand. When an adult makes a true request, the child has the option of saying "no" without getting into trouble.

Adults making requests are well-served to get into a frame of mind in which they are unattached to the result and can tolerate hearing "no" from the child. The goal is for the child to respond with a "yes" only if the child wants to say "yes." If the child wants to say "no," we would not want the child to say "yes" just to avoid punishment.

If the child says "no," we can gently seek further understanding of the child's needs related to the request. If we show an empathic understanding of what prevents the child from doing as we asked, then we can promote the likelihood of eventual cooperation. We can eventually seek an agreement that meets everyone's needs.

To further promote cooperation, it can be beneficial for children to participate in the creation of rules and agreements. Their participation helps to prevent resistance to abiding by these agreements.

One request that we can make to children with anger issues is to verbally express their frustration to us before taking matters into their hands (by striking someone, using profanity, or using any behavioral expression that leads to further difficulties). We can ask children (who are prone to anger problems) to tell us the feelings they are experiencing at such moments. In the classroom, the teacher can establish a nonverbal signal for the child to communicate the need for a moment with the teacher. This technique can allow for some privacy in the dialogue. Although this approach may be inconvenient to the teacher, the alternative is a child who loses self-control and has an outburst that is more disruptive than the verbalization of feelings. In this light, the inconvenience of the brief verbal exchange seems more satisfactory.

In some situations, especially in a classroom setting with many children, adults may find requests to be rather inefficient and inconvenient. We are better off deciding in advance whether we require immediate compliance or if we would merely appreciate the child's cooperation. When we are not in conflict with children and we have built rapport with them, commands or clear instructions may be appropriate in order to direct children to begin and end activities. We may also choose to give instructions if it is very important to the adult that the child immediately do something or if the child is engaged in a behavior that could cause harm to people or property. At such times, we can minimize the negative impact of commands by following a few guidelines: issuing the commands in a neutral or polite manner (even using the word please); making commands brief and uncomplicated; avoiding unnecessary verbalization after the command; and giving children at least five seconds to comply before we assume they are not complying.

In matters of physical protection, we must also sometimes make demands of children by setting limits on them. There may be some occasions when adults need to make decisions on behalf of the child. When children are using physical aggression, for example, we may need to use force to protect others. In other situations, as well, there may be times when we want to set limits to protect the rights and needs of others. In addition, we may sometimes need to protect children from themselves by setting limits on them. However, we can usually attempt to gain their cooperation well before the situation has reached this point.

Although it would be far better to limit the amount of control we exert over children, adults sometimes do not have the luxury of seeking cooperation. When control is necessary, we can minimize the negative impact on children by empathizing with their feelings related to our demand.

Have Fun Together

By engaging in pleasurable activities and having fun with our children, we can further our rapport with them, provide stress relief, and remind them that we value their need for fun. By accomplishing these things, we can help to keep their emotions on a more positive side. Furthermore, we can make it less likely that they will have anger reactions.

One valuable strategy to create fun, pleasurable experiences is through playful interactions with children. Toward that end, games and play can be used to create fun opportunities. When an adult and a child play games of the child's choice, the child usually enjoys the feeling that comes from choice. This is a simple way to balance the loss of power that children often feel in those instances in which adults must use their power over children.

During play, children can ideally choose from a variety of fun activities that are acceptable to the adult. The adult can enjoy the game as well. And the play allows the opportunity for the adult to model respectful behavior for the child.

In addition to play, we can provide other pleasurable experiences for children. Such experiences, of course, vary by age but can include going to the park, riding bicycles together, working on a puzzle together, going out for a meal or snack, going on a trip to the zoo or an amusement park, watching a movie or television show together, reading a story together, going to a sporting event together, or going boating or fishing.

In the school setting, pleasurable experiences can be created through playing classroom games. There are many books available on such classroom games. One example is the Great Group Games by Ragsdale and Saylor (2007). Classroom games can add student involvement to potentially tedious tasks like memorizing facts. Games also help people get comfortable with each other, create opportunities for learning, and allow children to practice social skills.

Encourage Contribution

Contribution is a basic need of humans. A rewarding experience, contribution comes naturally to us. It can be easier to see this if you think of how you feel when you do something for another person. The joy of contribution can also be taken away if it is forced upon us, and we are doing something out of a sense of obligation.

Children's contributions are sometimes taken for granted. And they are often pressured into doing things that they do not want to do. We can turn this around by helping children to experience their contributions as meaningful to us. We can do this by expressing our appreciation for their contributions. We can also begin to view the child's cooperative behavior as a form of contribution that we can appreciate and encourage.

Instead of simply thanking the child, we can report our feelings. We can also report the needs that are satisfied within us by the child's behavior. For example, "When I see that you cleaned your room, I am very relieved. Now I know you will be safe from tripping when you get out of bed in the middle of the night." Or, "I am thrilled by this gift from you, because I will have so much fun using it."

We can harness the power of the joy of contribution by letting our children know how much we appreciate it when they have peacefully expressed their frustration (i.e., without acting it out in ways that are problematic for us). To do this successfully, we must decide how we wish children to express their anger. Once we are clear on what types of statements and actions we prefer from children, we can then begin to encourage such behavior.

A good place to begin is to encourage children to verbalize upsetting feelings to us. When we notice the child has verbalized such feelings, we can express our appreciation for the child's contribution to the peacefulness of the environment. We speak to children about what we value in terms of their completed actions, rather than what we wish they would do. In other words, instead of focusing on negative behaviors, we notice as soon as they have expressed feelings. We then say that we are pleased with their self-expression. Although this process takes a little time and effort, I believe it is preferable to an anger outburst.

Each of three elements is important in using this process to effectively contribute to behavior change. We need to encourage immediately, repeatedly, and consistently. By doing so, we can provide (what behaviorists view as) positive reinforcement. To be more specific, we can best encourage children by letting them know their contributions as soon as possible after their actions. In addition, we can best encourage children by letting them know over and over again each time they contribute. Use of a nonverbal signal to accent the appreciation adds to the effectiveness of this process. Depending on the setting and the relationship, a handshake, high five, or thumbs up may be appropriate. We would show some enthusiasm even with older children as we encourage them. With younger children, it helps to add extra enthusiasm in our voices as we demonstrate our appreciation.

When children have well-established patterns of adaptive expression of their anger, we can begin to express our encouragement less consistently. However, we need to be consistent as we are helping them to develop new habits.

In contrast to our verbally appreciating the child's contribution (through our expression of our feelings and our satisfied needs), other statements may not have the same positive impact. Consider comments such as "Good job" or "You're fantastic." Even though these comments are positive, they do not inform children of the adult needs that were satisfied by the behavior. As a result, children may not know the important contributions that they have made.

When a child does not have the skills to perform the behavior of calmly expressing their feelings, we need to break this difficult task into smaller steps. By our expressing our appreciation of these smaller steps, the child will eventually perform the larger behavior. There are several ways to accomplish this task.

We can step in before the outburst has occurred and express appreciation for the child's self-restraint (even if the child would likely have lost their temper, seconds later). We can encourage the child by saying something like, "I am so pleased that you hesitated for a few seconds when you were angry. I know that one day you will even be able to calmly talk about your feelings of frustration and anger. I really value the peacefulness that you are working toward." We could also prompt children to report their feelings during moments of frustration, rather than waiting for them to report feelings on their own. Finally, we could encourage children when they remember to use their self-calming practices.

We can vary the way we express our encouragement of a child's contribution. We would not want the child to hear the same words over and over. We would like the child to hear the genuineness of our gratitude. For practical purposes, we may sometimes decide to shorten our verbal expressions of appreciation. We can still accomplish the objective by the following statement: "I am glad you used your calming breaths. Thanks for keeping the peace." In the example, notice the feeling of gladness and the need of peace.

What other behaviors could your children use as substitutes for the challenging behaviors they already tend to use? Taking each replacement behavior into consideration, can you identify any smaller steps that the child could perform to pave the way for this replacement behavior?

We want to give children much practice at performing these positive replacement behaviors and the smaller steps along the way to the full replacement behaviors. More practice means more opportunities for us to provide encouragement. Therefore, we have to allow children many situations in which they can show us what they are learning to do.

Contributions include more than just replacement behaviors for challenging behaviors. Contributions can include acts of service. Contributions can also include talents and interests that are used to add joy to the lives of others. Children's interests can be encouraged and nurtured, so that they see their potential gifts. If they enjoy art and it is encouraged and appreciated, children will come to use their art to contribute to others.

It can be beneficial to help children to develop a positive vision of the future. This vision provides hope and prevents despair, and it can be encouraged by adults who show enthusiasm for children's interests and strengths. Talking with children about their interests validates them and establishes rapport. Asking them what they want to be when grown up, or what their goals are, can stimulate a discussion of the ways they can contribute through their actions.

Lower Stress or Prepare for It

By keeping children from being overwhelmed with excessive stress, we make it less likely that they will experience anger. Although some stress is unavoidable and probably adaptive, it is important to realize when stress is becoming too great for children. Sometimes it is difficult to know where to draw the line. In the case of children who are prone to frequent displays of anger, it is especially important to be attentive to their stress levels.

As a simple example, we would not want to put pressure on these children to achieve straight A's in school. The stress could be too much, and the likelihood of an outburst would be increased. Of course, we can encourage effort and provide support to help the child achieve their potential.

Another example is refraining from overscheduling children with anger issues. On top of school, homework, and organized recreational activities, children need time for free play. Overscheduling them puts excessive stress on them.

Lowering demands to realistic levels is not the same as setting the bar low for the child. We can expect children to put forth effort, but we cannot expect everyone to excel in everything.

Can you think of any examples of excessive pressure on a child having anger issues? How can you help to lower the demands on the child?

We can prevent some stressful situations that are likely to overwhelm children. However, other stressful situations may be important for children to face. After all, if we avoid all stressful situations, we will miss out on many life opportunities. When we do not want children to miss out on important opportunities that may be stressful, we can help greatly by preparing children for the upcoming situation. In doing so, we can describe what is likely to happen, express our confidence in their abilities to meet the stress, practice the calming response that we have taught them, and discuss their concerns.

What stressful situations does your child need to face, without your lowering the demands? What can you say to the child to help prepare him or her?

Be a Problem-Solving Partner

Another preventive tool that we can provide to children is guidance in how to think through social problems. In her book on Interpersonal Cognitive Problem-Solving (ICPS, for short), Myrna Shure (1992) described the use of a process for teaching children to evaluate their own solutions to interpersonal problems. The process encourages children to come up with many possible ways that they could respond to problems that they are having with others. This brainstorming step allows children to consider all options that enter their minds.

For example, William can be helped to identify all the actions he could take if a peer were challenging him to a fight. In doing so, he should be encouraged to come up with as many options as he can. He identifies responses such as accepting the fight, trying to befriend the child, and telling a teacher at school.

Can your child identify a problem about which to brainstorm a variety of solutions? How many solutions can the child identify?

After these multiple options have been listed, we can teach children to consider each option one by one, including the consequences that are likely to go with each option. The child may come up with several possible responses, some better and some worse. For example, William may decide that the consequences of accepting the challenge to a fight could result in getting suspended from school, not to mention getting hurt. The consequences of telling a teacher at school could result in the children making peace or the other child getting angrier. On the other hand, the consequences of trying to befriend the other child, by calmly listening to the other child's issues, could result in peace between them.

After considering the possible consequences of the various potential solutions, the child can be helped to decide on a behavioral option. In our example, William may decide to try to befriend this other child.

If there was a recent behavioral episode, it can be useful to review the incident from a problem-solving perspective. This process involves reviewing the events that occurred before the child's behavior, the child's actual behavior that occurred, the consequences of the child's behavior, and other behavioral options that were available to the child (along with possible consequences of such options). Sometimes children also anticipate a difficult, upcoming interpersonal situation. At such times, they often need help in considering how to handle the situation.

This problem-solving process encourages a partnership between adults and children in discovering possible solutions, considering potential consequences, and deciding on future courses of action.

The ICPS curriculum would ideally be standard for children with chronic behavioral problems from anger, but other children could benefit from this curriculum as well. It is important to note that children are taught during times of peace, rather than during behavioral episodes. At times of peace, we are more able to consider alternatives.

Greene (2014) described, and illustrated in detail, a three-part problem-solving process that adults can use with children to address adult concerns about a child's behavior.

An initial step is for the adult to report his or her observations of the child's behavior. The adult also seeks an understanding of the child's perspective on the situation. The adult maintains a patient and curious attitude to encourage a full expression by the child.

After the child expresses his or her perspective, the adult expresses his or her own concerns related to the child's behavior. Finally, the adult encourages the child to work together to find a mutually satisfying solution to the problem.

To use a simplified example, let's suppose a child is having difficulty completing her homework. After the father reports his observations, the child's perspective is sought. The girl reveals that the homework is boring and that she would rather avoid it.

In this example, the father expresses a concern that the child will have difficulties on the test if she does not complete homework. Possibly the child's grade will be reduced as well for not doing the homework.

As the father invites the child to find a mutually satisfying solution, the girl identifies a solution to work for short periods of time with frequent breaks so that she can maintain enthusiasm. (The reader can consult Greene's book for additional examples and aspects of this process.)

Using concepts from NVC, we can also highlight the needs of the girl as part of the problem-solving process. The girl has an apparent need for mental stimulation (which is not satisfied by the homework). The father also helps the girl to identify her own needs for learning, growth, and challenge. Because her behavior involves avoiding the homework, her behavior is not satisfying the latter set of needs. By helping the girl to notice her unsatisfied needs, her father can help to motivate her to engage in a problem-solving process.

Along the way, we can use the ICPS steps of generating multiple solutions, evaluating possible consequences, and picking a solution.

By resolving these conflicts together, the child learns that the adult is a valuable resource and need not be viewed as a threat. This process contributes to the cooperation and mutual respect that minimize the likelihood of childhood anger outbursts.

Does your child demonstrate behaviors that you would like to bring to their attention? What words can you use to elicit the child's perspective on their behavior? After your child's perspective is expressed, how can you express your concerns to them? Finally, how can you invite the child to engage in a process of working together to solve the problem?

Chapter 8 Peaceful Parents Raise Happy Kids

Parenting is a task that requires a lot of responsibility. It is a life-long, fulltime job that no parent should neglect and should perform to the best of their abilities.

It's likely to happen that sometimes parents cannot fulfill their duties for whatever reason. They are also human after all, so they could be mentally distressed and may neglect their duties. This is completely natural, but a child won't be able to understand this situation. If a parent behaves this way, the child will be deeply affected, as will their upbringing.

In such cases, the child may grow up to develop a mental illness and won't be able to live life to the fullest. Their personality could become severely warped, making the child depressed, stressed out and dissatisfied. That is why it is of the utmost importance that parents understand their responsibility in not allowing this to happen to their children.

As a parent, you should try to keep a calm and peaceful attitude as you raise your children. In this section of the book, I'm going to talk about some of the tools that will help you in your role as a parent to handle your child's aggressive behavior while maintaining your inner peace.

Better Understanding

One of the most important reasons why you should try a peaceful approach for raising your child is the development of a better understanding between the two of you. One of the major issues that both parents and children have to deal with is a lack of understanding of one another. The very obvious generation gap between you is the main thing to try to overcome. A parent may not be able to immediately understand the way that the new generations, which their child is also a part of, think and act. A parent may try to restrict a behavior that is perfectly normal for the child, or might not be able to understand the things their child talks about.

In the same way, a child of a new generation will probably never understand the mentality, standards and molarity of their parents. Since they belong to older generations, and thus have a more "old-school" approach to life, children will have difficulty understanding where their parents are coming from.

In this situation, if parents become impatient and try to impose their beliefs on their children, it is quite likely that the child will rebel and refuse to follow their parents' guidance.

That's why it is so important for you to remain as calm as possible when dealing with your child. If you raise your children in a way that fosters peace, they will be more receptive to your point of view, and you will also be able to understand your child better.

Build Trust in Your relationship

Another huge benefit of a peaceful approach to parenthood is the trust that will develop between you and your child. Trust is one of the most important aspects in any kind of relationship. Think of it this way. Would you blindly follow a person you don't fully trust?

The same goes for children. As a parent, you are your child's first role model, their very first source of rules and guidelines for dealing with the world. If your child sees that you're always angry and stressed out, if you constantly yell at them and lose your temper around them, then your child will not be able to develop any kind of trust in you. They will prefer to stay away and not share their thoughts and feelings with you, rather than speak their mind confidently.

In this case, a peaceful attitude is extremely beneficial. If you give your child a safe space to share their issues with you and take the time to really listen to what they're saying, your child will naturally come to trust you. They will know that no matter what they're going through, you, as their parent, will listen and understand. This kind of trust is probably the most important aspect of a parent-child relationship.

Solving Problems with Ease

Another benefit that comes from peaceful parenting is that you will be able to solve problems with ease. It is impossible to solve any kind of problem in a satisfactory way when we are upset, stressed out or angry. Now imagine if your child comes to you for help while you're in that state of emotional turmoil. Would you be able to offer the best help you possible can? The answer is probably not. If you force yourself into problem-solving mode while you're upset, it is much more likely that you will make the situation even worse for everyone involved, including you and your child. This will, in turn, affect your whole family dynamic.

On the other hand, if you strive for a peaceful and calm state of mind, you will be able to handle problems more easily. Your mind will be at peak performance and the solutions you offer to any adversity will be much more efficient.

Treasure Special Moments

Yet another perk of a peaceful mind is that you will be able to truly treasure all those special moments with your child. When we find ourselves in constant emotional turmoil, we often miss the special moments that make our life precious. This also goes for all those wonderful moments you could be sharing with your child. Imagine that your child comes to you with some greats news of something that happened in school or with their friends. But you're having a pretty bad day yourself and you're in no mood for a noisy child, so you tell them to go to their room and leave you alone for a while. You will have missed out on a precious moment of your child's development and growth, as well as the chance to celebrate their victories with them. This is also something that will deeply wound your child.

Earn Respect

If your child sees that you always try to handle problems with a cool head and peaceful attitude, this will, in turn, increase the amount of respect your child has for you as the adult in their lives. Conversely, if you let your emotions get the better of you and constantly display aggressive behavior around your children, they will eventually want to stay away from the toxic environment of their home as much as possible.

If your child sees that you always try to handle problems with a cool head and peaceful attitude, this will, in turn, increase the amount of respect your child has for you as the adult in their lives. Conversely, if you let your emotions get the better of you and constantly display aggressive behavior around your children, they will eventually want to stay away from the toxic environment of their home as much as possible.

While we are not perfect by any means, it is important that our children see us not as disrespectful and angry adults. Rather, parents should strive to be a role model that their children respect and would proudly emulate when dealing with their own stressful situations. If your child sees that you remain calm under duress, that you tackle your problems head-on and sensibly and, above all, that you still show love and affection for your family, they will in turn adopt this kind of behavior as adults.

How to manage your anger?

As I have mentioned before, anger is a part of human nature. As such, it is impossible to avoid becoming angry, nor should you try to. There will always be situations that make us angry, just as there will always be situations that make us happy.

So, how can you become a parent that fosters peace and calm if you can't help getting angry sometimes? The best thing to do in this case is to manage your anger. It's perfectly valid to be angry, it's perfectly valid to be furious. But regardless of the intensity of your anger, you should do your best to keep it from spilling over to your parenting and affecting your child.

Here are some ways you can manage your anger and keep it from affecting your children.

Think before you speak

The golden rule of anger management: think before you speak. We often say things we don't mean when we're caught up in our own anger. We end up saying all the wrong things and hurting other people.

It is also very common that we shift the blame onto other people when we're upset and fail to see how we may also be responsible for creating a bad situation.

That's why it's so important that we make a habit out of thinking before we speak. Even taking as little as five deep breaths before responding can completely alter our state of mind. We will be able to see the situation more clearly, as well as become aware of the other person's point of view, which might be enough to defuse the situation.

Express your anger when you are calm

It is perfectly natural to want to express our anger the moment it is triggered, but this is not always the best approach. Blowing up at someone who made you angry can lead, again, to saying things you don't really mean, losing perspective of the situation, and damaging your relationship as a result.

This goes for your children too. If they do something that makes you angry and you immediately express that anger, you may end up blaming the child for all the wrong things, especially if the true reason for your anger is something else entirely, and your child was just the trigger. This not only hurts your child, but it teaches them that it's okay to act that way when they're angry.

Try, instead, to express your anger once you have calmed down. Practice the mindfulness exercises in previous chapters and only then, address the problem. You will surely see the situation under a different light and will have avoided escalating the situation into one where both you and your child would have ended up hurt by words spoken in anger.

Get some exercise

As mentioned before, exercise is a great way to manage difficult emotions like anger. Not only is it a diversion for your mind, but physical exertion can help you channel all that intense energy you feel when you're angry.

Try going out got a walk or a run or taking your anger out on a punching bag if you have access to one. Simply performing any kind of physical activity that appeals to you will improve your mood, as long as you enjoy doing it. Once you're done with your workout, you can return to handling the problem.

Take a timeout

Time-out isn't just for your kids! If the feelings of anger and frustration get to be too much, take a time-out yourself. Remove yourself from the problem for a while and perform any calming activities that you find enjoyable. Give yourself some time to think about the problem on your own timeframe, at your own pace. Once you've talked yourself down from the worst of your anger, you can leave your time-out and handle the problem.

Identify possible solutions

Finding a suitable solution to a problem that really angers you is not an easy task, since we can't think clearly when we're in that state of mind.

That's why it's best to try to come up with a solution only after you've calmed down a little. Instead of reacting to the problem, give the previous methods for calming yourself a try before trying to find a solution. Think about the possible outcomes of each solution you come up with and watch out for any course of action that you may be choosing as a result of your anger. Always choose the solution that best promotes the peace in yourself, your child and household.

Stick with "I" statement

Simply put, "I" statements are those that begin with the word "I". When arguing with someone else, you should always try to phrase your sentences in this way. Don't shift the blame onto the other person.

Compare these two sentences:

"You always leave the door open!"

And:

"I am upset because you always leave the door open."

While both sentences may be conveying a similar idea, they are in fact, quite different from one another. The first sentence is a complaint on something the other person is doing wrong according to you. In the second sentence though, you are communicating to the other person that you are upset without attacking them. According to several psychological studies, taking the time to phrase your sentences as "I" statements will help to reduce your anger.

Don't hold a grudge

Some people find it hard to let go of their anger when they feel someone has wronged them. The harder you hold on to a grudge, the harder it is to see things clearly and eventually find a solution to the problem. The grudge continues to fuel the anger until it becomes impossible to go about your day-to-day life without feeling consumed by those emotions.

If you work hard toward forgiving other people though, you will find yourself feeling lighter and much more relaxed in your everyday activities. This will also greatly improve your relationship with the people around you, including your children.

Use humor to release tension

Laughter really is the best medicine when it comes to stressful situations.

Sometimes it's tempting to let ourselves be swallowed by our negative emotions rather than put in the effort to get out of them. We will isolate ourselves and listen to sad songs when we're depressed, for example.

Next time you're under emotional duress, give humor a try. Watch a funny movie or TV show, look up funny videos on YouTube (there are *a lot*!) or call up a friend you can talk to about silly things. A good laugh is a perfect way to get you out of a rough emotional state and will give you a much-needed respite from the stress.

Practice relaxation techniques

I have talked about this in previous chapters, but relaxation techniques are always a great way to manage anger.

Aside from relaxation techniques, maybe you have a hobby that you haven't been able to indulge in since you became a parent. Try making some time to do things you truly enjoy doing, something that relaxes you and fills you with joy. Taking time for yourself is an important part of self-care and can greatly reduce stress, which in turn helps you to manage your anger much more easily.

If you don't have a hobby, try looking into things that interest you—this could be art, music, exercise, crafts, anything!

Know when to seek help

We all need a little outside help sometimes. The last thing you need is your anger damaging your personal, professional and social life, and potentially ruining your relationship with your children. If you find that your anger is too much to handle on your own, consider going to a professional. There is no shame in getting help, and the rewards you will gain from doing so will greatly exceed any misgivings you may have about it.

How to stop yelling at your child?

People who express their anger through yelling will sometimes blow up at a child who has angered them, even if they did so inadvertently.

The act of yelling at someone is never conductive to the resolution of the problem, but yelling at a child is even more problematic. Imagine, as before, a person three times taller than you, someone who is supposed to be looking out for you, suddenly yelling at you for doing something you didn't even know was wrong. This can have a very negative impact on your child. It is hurtful and will likely result in them becoming people who yell at others to vent their frustrations.

If you are the type of person that yells when angry, here are some more ways you can control your anger before it gets to the point where you start telling at your child.

Know your triggers

The need to yell at someone is something that rarely, if ever, appears out of nowhere. In all likelihood, your anger has been building over a certain period of time— shorter for some people than others—and then something will happen that triggers this reaction. If you have a child with ODD, then your child is probably a recurring trigger for your anger and you will end up yelling at them before you know what's happening.

That's why it is so important to know your triggers. Take a close at one incident where you lost your temper and yelled at your child. Examine the events leading up to the yelling and try to figure out what the trigger was. If you make it a habit of doing this, you will eventually be able to identify your triggers as they happen and stop yourself from yelling at your child before it happens. Over time and with patience, those triggers will lose their power over you and will no longer upset you to the point of yelling.

Give kids a warning

This works well when you already know your triggers. It's a good idea to give your child some warning about what behavior of theirs triggers your anger. If it's the kind of behavior that you wish to change, letting them know that it makes you angry can help in modifying it, which in turn prevents you from yelling at them.

If you're already angry and feel yourself about to start yelling, communicate your feelings of frustration to your child. If they're doing something that you don't wish to change in the long run, but rather just in that moment, tell them that what they are doing right now is making you uncomfortable or upset and ask them to stop for a while.

Make a Yes list

A Yes List is a list of things that you will commit to doing before you start yelling at someone. Take a pen and paper and write down this list. It could be anything from going to the bathroom and taking some deep breaths, to jogging in place, anything that takes you out of the situation. Put that list somewhere visible, like the fridge or a mirror so that you can look at it whenever you feel like you're about to start yelling. Perform one or more of the items on the list if you feel your temper rising.

Teach the lesson later

Under normal circumstances, the best time to teach your child a lesson if they did something wrong is right after the fact. If you have a short fuse though, it's a better idea to wait to impart wisdom until after you've calmed down. If you lose your temper and yell at your child after they make a mistake, it's unlikely that you're really thinking about teaching them anything. You're probably just venting your anger and shifting blame onto your child.

In this case, it's better that you follow the previous techniques for defusing your anger and getting your child to stop the activity that is making you angry. Once you've calmed down, it will be easier for you to communicate what bothered you about their behavior and for them to understand what you're trying to teach them.

Respecting your Child's Personality

In many ways, new generations are more advanced than their predecessors. Children today are fast-forwarding the evolution of humanity as a whole. If adults took the time to listen to what they have to tell us and to patiently answer their questions, we could see in their words the wisdom acquired over many generations.

In particular, there is a certain tendency toward more emotional responses from children of newer generations than there was in the previous ones. Our parents (and *their* parents) would never have even dreamed of talking back to an authority figure at home or at school like children do today. Expressing emotions rather than keeping them bottled up is incredibly necessary for a child to grow into a balanced and happy adult. Letting our children do this and learning from them is the best way to move forward as a society.

It's not easy to overcome years (and generations) of repressed emotions. But if we look at our children, listen to what they have to say and, particularly, try to identify what we find most annoying about the attitude, we will learn a valuable lesson about ourselves. If, for instance, you feel like your child doesn't show you your due respect, perhaps consider that you're not showing your child the same respect you want to receive. Many times, a certain behavior or attitude that annoys us about someone else, especially our children, is only a reflection of something that we dislike about ourselves.

Another example is when a parent tries to impose their way of doing things to their children. A child or teenager may already have their preferred way of doing something, but a parent insists they do it their way because "that's how things are done" or "because I said so". In an ODD child, or a rebellious teenager, this will cause them to tell you to back off and mind your own business. Children and teenagers are also entitled to making their own decisions and if what they are doing isn't causing them or anyone else any harm, take a step back and let your child do their thing. It's important for you to remember that a child is not yours to control, but rather try to see the world through them and their experiences.

"Should I just let my children do whatever they want then?" I hear you asking. Well, yes and no. If what they want to do is not hurting them or the people around them or illegal, then yes. Let your child do their thing, be who they want to be, and express themselves freely.

A parent may not always like a certain aspect of their child's personality, but have to respect it nonetheless.

Let's say, for example, that Lily is messy teen. She has the habit of always leaving her things all over the floor. Rather than getting angry and demanding that she pick up after herself, you could try asking her why she prefers to leave her things strewn about rather than picking them up. Does she feel safe and comfortable in a messy room rather than a clean one? If the answer is genuinely "yes", then you can tell her that you're the opposite— that you don't feel comfortable in such an environment. Then you can try to reach a compromise. You can tell her that as long as she keeps the common areas in the house tidy, she can keep her room however she likes.

This will promote the peace between you, since you won't have a reason to be angry at the mess in her room and she will make the effort to be tidy in other areas of the house.

Your relationship with your child is bound to change once you open yourself up to the idea of learning about your child's personality and trying to accept the aspects of it that you don't really like. Do not be afraid of sharing these thoughts with your child! If they see you making an effort to meet them halfway, they will respond in kind. They will grow to become adults who know that they are free to be themselves and who are confident about their life choices.

If you find that your child shows little or no interest in exploring the world, cannot find a hobby and has no desire to be independent or autonomous, you should step in as their parent to offer help. The very first step is to reinforce your bond with your child, show them affection without them having to ask or fight for it. Let them feel relaxed in their relationship with you.

Here are some tips you can follow to help your child discover their hidden potential.

Tip No.1 – Give your child affection

Hug your child, tell them you love them and will always take care of them. This is especially important before parting, when you send your child to school or to an unfamiliar place.

Be encouraging of your child's thoughts, ideas and passions. Words like "it's amazing that you did this all by yourself!" is preferable to "I like what you did!".

Tip No.2 - Give your child space to self-teach

Give your child a chance to try to understand the essence of things by themselves. Don't try to force them into early development. A child who has known the incredible feeling of discovering something by themselves will develop a self-sufficient personality later on. Unfortunately, most of today's children do not have luxury to feel the excitement of a new discovery—the Internet already provides all the answers before they even know to ask the questions.

Try to create opportunities for your child to learn something new by themselves, away from outside influences or pressures.

Tip No.3 - Give your child time for free play

As mentioned before, your child needs time for free play, away from school, homework, and organized recreational activities. You have shown affection to your child and created a space for them to learn new things. Now it's time to just let your child do their own thing and for you to sit back and watch. How much time do they spend on an activity? How long do they think and plan before doing something—drawing, stacking blocks, dancing, etc.?

If your child gets bored too quickly, try not to be swayed into immediately playing with them. Some parents will bend over backwards trying to keep their child entertained at all times. If you've already spent time playing with your child and feel like you need to step back, let them find ways to entertain themselves. Try telling them: "I'll be right here for, I'm not going anywhere, but I can't play with you right now."

Tip No.4 - Give your child control and responsibilities

If you give your child a chance to steer the wheel and make their own decisions, they will slowly learn that they are in control of their life and will strive to realize their potential. Provide your child with an environment in which they are able to safely express their will. Give your child autonomy whenever possible. Ask them what they want to wear rather than picking out clothes for them. Let them decide what they want to have for breakfast or what time they want to go to bed. Trust that your child will make the right decisions for themselves and let them handle some responsibility—ask them to make lunch for the family or assign them some of the house chores.

Your role as a parent is to determine how much freedom to give your child and in what areas of their lives—where to relinquish some of your control, or all of it. It is up to you to decide when your child is ready to handle being in control and in charge of more responsibilities.

Chapter 9 Solutions to Solve Their Stubborn Behaviors

Growing teens find it hard to communicate freely with their parents. As a parent, you need establish an open line of communication to avoid problems that may arise due to the aforementioned generation gaps. Keeping an open and honest communication also ensures that your child does not develop aggressive behavior.

The relationship between a parent and their child is a really special one. When they're little, children depend completely on their parents for care, security and love. They naturally see their parents as their best friends, their protectors and confidantes. They depend on their parents to love and support them without judgment, regardless of their mistakes and shortcomings. As a parent, it is your responsibility to be a source of emotional stability for your child.

As your child grows into a teenager, they may begin to exhibit aggressive behaviors. Their feelings become more complex and they suddenly find that they lack the words to communicate their thoughts and needs to their parents. This can lead to miscommunication and fights between you and your child.

Teenagers want to become adults, and they want to do it fast! This can be stressful for them as they are only just building their self-identity and learning to deal with the outside world. These are trying times for your child— they feel lost and vulnerable even though they try to put up a tough front.

It is a normal phenomenon that a teenager's mind becomes filled with confusion, conflict, doubts, anxiety, and other negative feelings. As your child goes through this tough time in their life, it is your responsibility as a parent to establish a channel of communication with them. Help them to put their thoughts and feelings into words, provide a safe space for them to do so, let them know that what they are going through is normal. Unless you create the right space at home for them to be able to express themselves, your teen will remain closed off and you will become a mere spectator in these difficult times.

In order to make parenting a teenager a little bit easier, try to curb your expectations. Try to accept your teen's passions (even if you do not fully understand them). Do not try to manage your teen, let them do their own thing. Try parenting courses and find things that both you and your teenager can enjoy doing together.

Adopting the Paradigms of Highly Effective Parents

If you want your child to develop a positive attitude, you have to first adopt the paradigms of the highly effective parents, which can be summarized as follows:

Kids' Model of the World is different from that of the Parents

As a parent, the starting point is to change your mentality in regards your world model. You first need to understand and acknowledge that your view of the world is not the same as your child or teen's view. You shouldn't try to impose your views on them. What may seem to you like sage, worldly advice, may just seem like nagging to your teen and they may feel like you're trying to control them.

Parenting a teenager requires a lot of understanding, tolerance, humility and patience. In some ways, this is probably the most challenging period you will face as a parent. Even so, parenting a teenager doesn't have to be a terrible experience. Here are some techniques you can apply to make parenting your teenager easier and more enjoyable for you.

Technique 1: How to Develop a Method to Raising Children

Some parents seem to be so successful in raising children to be responsible, caring and honest adults, while many others just can't seem to get it right. First, it is important to realize that your responsibility as a parent is to help your children to develop a good, strong moral character. This is something that doesn't just magically happen; it takes a great deal of effort, time and focus.

There are a number of parenting tips that will be very useful and valuable when it comes to helping your teen develop a strong character that will help them in the years to come. If you have a parenting partner however, it won't matter how great these techniques are if you don't work together as a team.

Your partner should always be in your corner and you should always be in theirs. This requires that you establish communication and regularly discuss the values you want to instill in your children, as well as the best approach to achieve this. When it comes to discipline, love and their upbringing, team effort and constant communication will ensure that you and your partner are both on the same page.

When the going gets rough, as it inevitably will, sometimes having a few extra ideas up your sleeve can really make life a whole lot easier—for kids and parents alike. This is also something that requires full commitment from the parenting figures in the child's life. Here are a few more tips that have worked wonders for many parents.

Tip #1: Teach, Discuss & Demonstrate Valuable Traits

As a parent, you must be a firm believer in discussing with your child what is appropriate behavior and what isn't. But just talking about it isn't enough. If you talk the talk, you've got to walk the walk, as the saying goes.

So, while it is important to talk to your child about the importance of being patient, for example, by explaining why we have to wait our turn at the grocery store or to go on a ride at an amusement park, it's equally important for you not to lose your cool when you're in a hurry and find yourself forced to wait as well.

Tip #2: Help Your Child Learn Responsibility

Chores are a must when it comes to helping your child learn the valuable lesson of responsibility. Providing your child with tasks on a regular basis is a great way of teaching self-reliance and encouraging pride in a job well done.

When your child has finished their task, make sure to acknowledge their efforts with, a hug, a thumbs-up or a pat on the back. Always remember to tell them how much you appreciate the job they've done and how much they have helped you out.

Tip #3: Use Praise... and Be Specific!

Praising your children when they demonstrate positive character traits is a great way of reinforcing those characteristics you hope to develop.

For example, if helping your child to learn how to be a good friend and value strong friendships is important to you, making a practice of offering them specific praise is an excellent place to start.

It's only human to want to do more of the things we get positive feedback on. So when your child is understanding or does something kind or polite, make a point of letting them know what you think.

Honesty is another positive trait that can be encouraged using the right language. When your child is honest about something they have or haven't done, acknowledge their honesty without reprimand by saying something along the lines of: I like the way you were honest about not finishing your homework. Let´s sit down and see what still needs to be done so you can finish it now.

Tip #4: Be the Best Role Model

Of course, the best way to help your child develop positive character traits is to mirror those traits in your own behavior as well. You are, after all, your child´s number one role model.

You must decide and vow to be the best example of those traits that you value most and want to instill in your child. If you make a habit out of practicing them, your child will surely notice—maybe not consciously at first, but rest assured that your actions will most definitely have a positive effect on a deeper level.

As you practice each of these parenting tips, know you are doing more than just raising a well-behaved child. You are raising a responsible, caring individual with a strong sense of right and wrong.

Helping your child develop a strong moral character isn´t always easy but it is tremendously rewarding. After all, these are values and skills your child will benefit for the rest of their lives!

Technique 2: How To Understand Your Child Better

It's likely that after some time you will come to know what to expect from your child. But knowing what to expect from your teen is not enough—you have to take it one step further: you have to reach out and into their own world. This requires you to be able to understand them, understand their language, their points of view, and the problems they face on a daily basis and knowing what they want from you as a parent.

What are the Top Five Things the Teens Expect from Parents?

1. Being Loved and Accepted

2. Being Recognized and Validated

3. Freedom and Independence

4. Being Trusted

5. Being Respected

Understanding your teen can be a daunting task at times. Your conversations may degenerate to name calling, loud arguments and miscommunication most of the time. Rather than feeling miserable which only serves to perpetuate the pattern, focus on understanding what makes your child tick. Once you learn to communicate with them and acknowledge their feelings, it will be easier to understand them and go a step further to develop a long-lasting and productive relationship with them.

Tip #1: Maintain an Open Communication with Your Teen

You need to reconsider how you communicate with your teen. Is your communication centered on commands, complaints, and punishment? Do you have an open communication in which you allow them to air their views and feelings freely? You will not be able to understand your child if you don't encourage them to talk.

You should be the one to start the conversation with an open-ended question. Ask your child or teen how their day in school was and continue asking more open-ended questions to encourage them to talk. If they're not in the mood, just let them know you are ready to listen to them when they feel ready.

Take advantage of the times you share together, like when you're in the car or setting the table for dinner, to open communication with them. Pay close attention to what they're saying and show genuine interest in their likes and passions. The main goal of this approach is simply to understand what motivatives your child and makes them happy. It is about getting to understand their aspirations and inspirations.

Tip #2: Acknowledge Your Child's Feelings

It is important that your child knows that what they feel matters to you as a parent. They might get angry, frustrated or embarrassed sometimes. Instead of brushing them off and telling them to stop overreacting, offer the support they need.

It is advisable to allow your child to talk when you are in a heated discussion. It is important that you listen to them, nod and maintain eye contact. If possible, you can even repeat what they said as a sign that you are actually listening and acknowledging their feelings. A hug is a magic and powerful thing that you may find very useful at times too.

Tip #3: Respect Your Child's Need for Independence

Every time your teen challenges your authority, it is important to understand that they are simply trying to demonstrate their independence. You have to keep in mind that your child is growing both physically and mentally. For them, this is the start of their independence.

This requires that you consider being flexible and give up a little control As mentioned before, it's a good idea to let them pick their own clothes, for example—both when shopping for new ones and when selecting what to wear for the day.

Independence also means respecting your child's privacy. If you didn't do so before, consider knocking before entering their room, asking for permission to come in, and giving them some time alone. Keep an eye out if your child seems to be spending too much time alone though. If your child seems withdrawn, take the time to talk to them and ask if they have a problem they would like to talk about.

Tip #4: Understand How the Brain of a Teen Works

As a parent, you need to understand that the brain of a teenager is in a constant state of change. Once you recognize and appreciate this fact, you are more likely to understand and accommodate their behaviors. Because different parts of the brain mature at different rates, your teen's reactions might seem irrational to you.

In reality, the part associated with reward and motivation and impulsiveness matures much earlier than the part of the brain that is associated with the task of weighing the pros and the cons of every given action.

Consequently, your teen does not have the same view of the consequences of their actions as you do. With this in mind, it will be helpful that you discuss with your child the risk factors associated with risky decisions.

Technique 3: How To Orient And Guide Your Child To Make The Right Choices

Culture is the way of life of a given community. It relates to the socially transmitted habits, traditions, customs, and beliefs that are unique to a group of people at any given time.

More often than not, teenagers are likely to be left behind in catching up with the norms, values, behavior patterns, practices, etiquette, social groups, religion, superstitions, and spirituality among several other cultural concepts. There are several guides that can be helpful when orienting your teen into the cultural path you think might be best for them—always keeping in mind that they will ultimately make this choice for themselves.

Remain observant of your teen's behavior, their performance in school and their relationships with their peers, friends, teachers and other people in their inner circle. This, along with an open channel of communication, should help you to understand what problems your teen might be facing in regards to the world around them.

If their behavior seems different than normal in a way that is affecting them negatively, go back to the basics and try to re-establish communication with them. Find ways to get your teen to open up to you and talk to you about their problems. Getting a teen to open up is no easy feat, but by employing the right techniques (being friendly, listening to them without judgment, offering support, etc.) it is certainly an attainable goal.

Once your child has opened up to you and told you what problems they're facing, then it's time to offer some advice. Express to them what choice you think is the best one for them, but always take the time to explain *why* you believe that choice to be the right one for *them*.

The Right Choices

Your teen needs to understand that their choices must always be in compliance with the provisions of local laws and regulations. Any illegal activities must be explained to them as such, as well as the consequences of taking part in them.

Situations you may have to deal with:

Situation #1: When Your Child Hasn't Come to a Decision

If your child or teen doesn't know what choice to make in any given situation, the one thing you absolutely must not do is try to impose your views on them. Instead, make time for the both of you to analyze your child's problem and lay out what you consider to be the best solution or course of action to follow.

Consider comparing different solutions to a problem and try to explain the consequences or benefits that each of those solutions could carry. The most important thing is not to force your child to make a choice—let them mull over each potential solution, analyze the outcome and ultimately make their own decision.

Situation #2: When Your Child Has Decided on a Course of Action

In some cases, your teen may already have made up their mind about how to solve a problem they're facing and all that's left is for them to carry out their decision. In that case, it's your role as a parent to show your love and support and offer to help them carry out their choice if they need it. This vote of confidence on your teen will make them feel trusted and will ensure that they come to you for their future problems.

Technique 4: How To Help Your Child Break Down The Wall That Separates Them From Family And Society

Feeling "alone in a room full of people" is an exceedingly common emotion among teenagers. Your teen may start to feel like they don't fit in anywhere, which is a huge source of distress at this age. Teens need to feel like they belong and fit in with the word around them in order to get a sense of security and safety.

When your teen tells you "I don't fit in", what they're trying to say is "I don't feel safe". They feel different and alienated, which turns to anxiety. While this issue is likely more common in the school setting, teens can experience this feeling anywhere, even at home.

As a parent, you can do a lot to change the family environment—everything this book has talked about so far will help with that—but the truth is you can't make society adapt to your child. No matter how much you may want to change the world to fit them, the only thing you can do is to work with your child and give them the social skills necessary to help them cope with this feeling of isolation.

Skill #1: Ensure That Your Child Feels Loved and Supported at Home

When teenagers feel rejected by their family, they tend to exhibit defiant behaviors. As such, as a parent of a teenager, you need to pay closer attention to your child and focus on understanding their feelings and desires.

Other good ways to help your child feel included in the family is to organize activities that everyone participates in, like weekly family meetings, parties, or picnics. It is important that every member of the family participates in equal measure. This way, your teen will be exposed to the importance of family unity and it enables them to enjoy some much-needed solidarity, fun, attention and love from family.

Skill #2: Teach Your Child to Be a Good Friend

There is no doubt that friendship is a crucial aspect of any child's development and growth. It is through playing and misunderstandings with friends that children learn skills like sharing, compromising, problem solving, forgiving, and most other social skills.

Teach your child empathy from an early age by being helpful in social events, making birthday cards for friends and family members, offering a helping hand to the those younger than they and to the elderly. The skills they learn at home will naturally extend out into the world.

Skill #3: Tune into Your Child's Friendship Style

Some children thrive in large groups of friends, while others feel more comfortable with one or two kids at a time. It's crucial that you understand what works best for your child and not force them into social situations they find uncomfortable.

Keep in mind that what works for you may not necessarily work for them. If your child is happy playing with one friend, let them be and don't force them to go to a big birthday party if it upsets them.

Skill #4: Open Your Home to Your Child's Friends

Make sure your child knows that your home is open to their friends. When they're younger, you can arrange play dates and have some activities prepared for them.

As your child begins to shift into adolescence, they will want to plan their own activities with their friends, but this doesn't mean they can't still go to your home. Let your teen know their friends are welcome any time and give them privacy and a safe space to have their fun.

Skill #5: Help Your Child Work through Family and Friendship Troubles

Misunderstandings are common among family members, friends and peers. Your teen may need help from time to time in working through the emotions that arise from such conflicts. As private as teens tend to be, they may not immediately tell you about a fight or misunderstanding with a friend. Keep an eye out for any signs that your teen is distressed and try approaching them about it.

Depending on the severity of the conflict, your teen may even consider ending a friendship after a fight. In this case, it is not your role to step in and solve things for them. Rather, teach them the skills necessary to work through such situations. Draw on your own experience to show them that everyone fights sometimes, but that it is important to listen to the other person's side of the argument and try to be understanding. Explain the importance of not making rash decision in the heat of the argument, and that it is preferable to wait until they've calmed down to try and solve the issue.

Skill #6 Encourage Your Child to Take Part in Extra-Curricular Activities

A great way to help a teen who is feeling isolated is to encourage them to engage in activities they enjoy. This could be anything from sports clubs to music or art programs—in school our out. This way, your child will be able to feel connected to other people their age who enjoy the same things.

Skill #7: Call in the Experts

If you believe that your teen's feelings of isolation and alienation are a matter for concern, don't hesitate to seek help from professionals. If not addressed early, severe feelings of isolation can result in depression and low self-esteem.

Technique 5: How To Put Yourself In Your Child's Position To Understand Them Better

During these trying years, your teen will be fighting many different battles at once. The best thing you can do as their parent is to offer support and understanding and show them that you're there for them. Try as best as you can to put yourself in their shoes. We were all teenagers once after all, and know full well what it's like to be in that position. Try to remember the things you wanted, thought and felt when you were a teenager and keep that perspective close to your heart when helping your teen.

Remember that teenagers need help in learning how to manage their emotions. Don't lose your temper at your teen's emotional outbursts. Rather, try to keep your cool in order to make it easier to solve the conflict.

Your Teen Needs Space to Develop Their Personality

After a certain age, your teen will start to undergo a very rapid process of development. All the physical changes that are clearly visible are only the tip of the iceberg— it's the psychological changes that form the bulk of their developmental changes.

Provide Support

Be supportive by letting your teen develop their own personality and go through their own process of self-discovery. There are several occasions where your teen's emotions will overcome their better judgment. When that happens, allow them to vent their frustrations until they calm down. You do have to establish boundaries, however—if you don't tolerate name-calling, for example, this can be a good place to draw the line of what is allowed during their outbursts.

Being a teenager is not easy. This is a time where your child needs a lot of support from you. It is common to have a love-hate relationship with teens at times, but by offering your love and support, you will be on the right track to helping them get through these rough years.

Chapter 10 Strategies to Manage and Control Students with Oppositional Defiant Disorder (ODD)

The first characteristic of ODD is that the behavior of those who have this disorder does not go as far as breaking the law. Children with ODD may refuse to do schoolwork, follow the rules at home or at school, and be disrespectful of adults, but they will not break the law.

In another book in this series we will examine Conduct Disorders (CD), which do involve behaviors that violate our moral values and sometimes breaks the law as well. Children and adolescents with Conduct Disorders lie, cheat, steal, vandalize property, start fights deliberately looking to hurt other people, harm animals, and are often indifferent to the impact of their behavior on others.

The second characteristic is that the roots of Oppositional Defiant Disorder run deep in the families of the children who have it. Children do not develop ODD simply because they are mismanaged or there is some moderate degree of stress in a household.

The third defining characteristic of ODD refers to the trigger of this disorder in a child, namely a difficult family environment.

A note about the relationship between family problems and ODD behavior

The majority of children who display oppositional and defiant behavior do not actually have ODD. Rather, their opposition and defiance are caused by other factors.

For example, imagine that you teach eighth-grade math and Mike is a student of yours with a learning disability who struggles terribly to do work at grade level. You believe the best course of action is for this Mike's parents to sit with him every day for half an hour to review and do his math assignments. This will not make the Mike's learning disability to go away, but it will benefit him greatly.

Every evening though, when it's time to sit down with his parents, he runs out the back door and does not come home until bedtime. In this case, Mike is a student who is oppositional and defiant. But he doesn't have an

Oppositional Defiant Disorder; he has a learning disability, which makes math hard for him and, in turn, makes him hate it. While there are other ways to help children with problems like this, it won't do them any good to be labeled with an ODD that clearly does not exist.

Consider also the example of Sarah, a fifth-grade student with Attention Deficit Hyperactivity Disorder (ADHD) who cannot get her work done in the course of a normal school day. Her teacher sends home a note every day, listing all the incomplete work with the hopes that Sarah's parents will sit with her for an appropriate period of time and try to get some of that work done. When Sarah's parents ask her about school though, she lies and tells them that she doesn't have any homework for the day because she got it all done at school.

When the truth comes to light, as it inevitably must, Sarah might react with defiance and opposition. But, again, this isn't an indication of ODD—Sarah is behaving this way because her ADHD makes it impossible for her to sit still and focus on school work.

First Things First

Never allow your students to draw you into a conversation about fairness. It is a trap and an argument you can't win. This is because it is very difficult for children to make the distinction between treating people fairly and treating them equally.

As a teacher, it is important to establish from the outset that cannot and will not treat everyone equally. You might say to your class, "Every one of you will get from me what you need to succeed academically. However, what you need to be successful may not be the same as what the person sitting next to you needs. It wouldn't be fair for me to treat everybody the same when everyone's needs are different."

You can then offer some examples of this in the classroom. For example, if a student is having trouble understanding a new concept, take some extra time to explain it to them again. Or if a student is quick to catch on and finishes their work early, you can find some other activity for them to do while they wait for their peers.

You might not want to go quite as far as the teacher who responded to a student's complaint, that something wasn't fair by saying, "the fair comes to town only once a year and today's not the day."

There is nothing wrong with explaining to your students that some of them have special needs that require that they be treated differently than others. We will not violate their privacy, of course, but we can talk to the class about student behavior in general ways that make clear where priorities lie.

Managing parents who feel their child has been treated unfairly is another matter and, although most parents are responsive to a supportive teacher's explanations, quite often, angry parents require the participation of the principal or other professionals in the school to help them understand why their child is being treated the way they are.

It is fair to say that if you get caught up in an argument about whether something is fair, you've already lost the battle.

General Principles of Behavior Management

Whether you are working with students with ODD, ADHD or any other type of behavior problem, there are some basic principles of behavior management that sometimes get lost in the hustle and bustle of a busy classroom.

1. Pick your battles. Not everything that is a problem needs to be confronted. Ask yourself if it is worth the time and energy.

2. Plan in advance. You cannot anticipate everything that will go wrong with your students during the year, but you know the general types of problems you will face and you need to have planned for them before they occur.

3. Have a crisis management plan in place. This is not a plan to change the child's behavior in the long run, it is a plan on how you will deal with an urgent matter such as explosive anger or a student who swears at you or is openly defiant and challenging in the presence of other students. Crisis management is a school-wide responsibility.

4. Second chances should be used carefully. The purpose of a second chance is to give the child the opportunity to learn from the first experience and demonstrate that they have learned the cognitive and the behavior elements of the lesson. But second chances quickly become a lesson with unintended consequences for teachers. Second chances used routinely are a good way to teach the lesson that you always get one misbehavior for free. Second chances also put the emphasis on

control coming from the teacher. The more we are the ones who prescribe proper behavior, the less emphasis there is on the students thinking through an act before they commit it.

5. Remain calm.

6. Zero tolerance policies always work against you in the long run. They seem to be the fairest way to manage serious problems, but since circumstances differ so much between two students who do the same thing, the zero-tolerance policy eventually makes students as well as members of the community lose respect for our ability to think clearly about behavior problems. It is reasonable to have zero-tolerance policies for certain behavior in relationship to consequences. It is foolhardy to dispense punishment without critical thinking.

7. Out-of-school suspension usually makes problems worse. In-school suspension is only a little bit better. Suspension out of school is effective for two reasons. First, sometimes it is necessary to remove a student for short period of time from the classroom or the school in order to give them time to settle down and let the rest of the students calm down as well.

Second, there are times that suspension is the only way teachers and administrators can get parents' attention.

No one likes to say it directly in public, but many educators know that the only way to get parents involved in a child's problems in some cases is to force them to face the consequences of their own behavior. That might mean losing a few days' pay as they are forced to take time off from work and attend to their child. What suspension does not do is change the student's behavior.

8. Action changes behavior, not words.

9. Do not ask children or teenagers why they have misbehaved.

10. Do not give lectures about the importance of education, honesty, or proper behavior. No one underachieves or lies because their parents or teachers have forgotten to tell them to act properly. All this does is demonstrate to the student that you do not really understand them at all and it diminishes the likelihood that you will be able to build effective productive relationships with them.

11. Do not make idle threats or promises.

12. If you have imposed a punishment or the child is facing certain consequences, it is OK to allow the student to earn their way back into your good graces, but only

in certain specific circumstances when you can be certain that the problem will not happen again. It is a modified second chance.

13. If you have a rule for your classroom do not debate it or compromise. If you were not certain in the first place that it was a good rule, then have a discussion with your students at that time and modify the rule if it seems like a good idea, but once in place, it stays.

14. Do not be afraid to be wrong. Every once in a while you will punish someone unfairly or you will blame someone who is not at fault or your punishment may be too lenient or too severe. We try to avoid these circumstances, but they happen and if you worry too much about them they will cripple your efforts at classroom management and undermine your self-confidence. No one is seriously harmed by these types of mistake although there is serious harm in hesitating too much because you are uncertain that students lose respect for your ability to manage the classroom and learn how easily you can be manipulated.

15. Avoid the bad habit of asking questions that begin with the words, "How can I get this student to...?"

You cannot get anyone to do anything. All you can do is alter your own behavior in ways that will influence the other person. This is more than playing games with semantics. Too often we focus on the other person and give up in frustration when we cannot get them to comply with our way of doing things. The focus has to be on our own behavior. Ask instead, "What can I do to influence this student to behave?" and you will be heading in the direction of constructive strategies.

16. Do not spread your efforts too thin.

Chapter 11 Communication

What is communication? Communication is the way human beings send verbal and nonverbal messages (or both) from one person to another.

It is important to note the difference between the verbal messages we send to one another, and the nonverbal ones. Let's examine the differences between the two.

Verbal communication is defined as the actual words people use to speak. You may or may not be aware of this, but verbal communication only makes up 10 percent of the messages we send to one another. In actuality, 90 percent of the messages we send back and forth requires no words at all! This is called nonverbal communication.

Nonverbal communication is defined as sending messages back and forth to one another without words. These messages are sent to others through:

Eye contact

Facial expressions

Voice tone

Voice volume

Rate of speech

Silences/pauses

Hand gestures

Body positioning

Body distance

The most successful people on the planet have the ability to tap into the 90 percent of communication that really reaches and leads people. If I had the choice to understand and apply verbal communication skills vs. nonverbal communication skills, I would prefer nonverbal!

Why? Because if communication (verbal and nonverbal) was given as a test, I would rather receive a 90 percent and get an A! How would you want to score?

Let us examine these nine powerful ways we send messages to one another including our children. With this newfound knowledge, the current way you look at parenting your child will change forever!

I am about to show you how to tap into the nonverbal form of communication, so you can be aware of what is really going on around you.

Eye contact

Examine any fight, argument, or disagreement. What is the first thing that goes between two people?

Eye contact!

There is just no way around it. When someone doesn't want to talk about the same subject or doesn't want to do what another person is doing, they will look away immediately.

Why does this happen? In short, looking into another person's eyes is very intimate and personal. For some reason, it is extremely hard to look someone in the eye and be upset with the person at the same time.

Do you think you can look into someone's eyes and be upset with them for an extended period of time? Try it. The next time you are upset with your child, or anyone for that matter, make yourself look them in the eyes.

Notice if they are looking back. Monitor how long you both stare into each other's eyes before the negative feeling goes away.

I'd give it thirty seconds to one minute tops! You won't be able to help feeling reconnected with them, just through eye contact.

How can you use this nonverbal tool to your advantage? Simply look at your child to see if they are still looking at you. Long before they throw a tantrum or start to become difficult, they will look away. Use this as an indicator of their current state and to reestablish a connection with them, by initiating eye contact.

Facial expressions

Just like eye contact, facial expressions are powerful ways to communicate nonverbally! In fact, even if your child is not making eye contact, you still have the ability to be "in tune" with them by looking at their facial expressions.

This is because whether children are happy, sad, angry, afraid, excited, frustrated, embarrassed, surprised, worried, jealous, disappointed, hurt, sorry, ashamed, proud, enraged, interested, disgusted, joyous, or in awe, it is almost impossible to completely mask how they feel during that moment.

How do you use this nonverbal tool to your advantage? Simply stop what you are doing, and take the time to look at their facial expressions.

As you do this, do not try to change their feelings, simply voice what you see ("You look angry"). This will encourage them to talk with you instead of continuing to stay quiet or closed off emotionally.

Voice tone

Voice tone is an interesting way to communicate nonverbal messages to others, because you can make one statement and the statement can have several meanings. This is achieved by the words you choose to emphasize with your tone of voice.

Voice tone communicates nonverbally how a person feels emotionally. Voice tone can also communicate nonverbally what a person thinks about something, and what they plan to do about it.

How do you use this nonverbal tool to your advantage? By monitoring your own tone of voice, and stating your words as matter-of-factly as possible, you will be teaching your children how to be calm, cool, and collected when things don't go their way.

Voice volume

Voice volume is another interesting way to communicate nonverbal messages to others because it communicates that we were not heard or understood. We are repeating ourselves in a louder volume to be heard!

Usually a person will use a louder voice volume if they doesn't feel heard, or if they were purposefully ignored.

Voice volume communicates nonverbally how a person feels emotionally. It especially communicates excitement, happiness, anger, frustration, rage, jealousy, pride, or disgust with others. Voice volume is also used as a power move to interrupt or control other people, by talking over them.

How do you use this nonverbal tool to your advantage? By monitoring your own voice volume and speaking lower, others will follow. Remember, it takes two people to have a shouting match. Simply, the next time your children (or anyone) are yelling at you, deliberately lower your voice, and watch how long it takes for them to stop shouting. I'd give it thirty seconds, and they will follow your lead.

Rate of speech

The rate of speech is defined as how fast or how slowly a person speaks to another. Rate of speech can communicate nonverbally either in-depth knowledge or pure uncertainty about any subject matter. It can also communicate nonverbally the patience or impatience the speaker has with the person listening.

When a person knows the ins and outs of a particular topic, they may have an increased rate of speech because they have mastered that subject matter. The person is not tripping over their words because they have sufficient practice and expertise.

On the other hand, someone may speak extremely fast to act as if they have such mastery; but when you take a closer look, the person really doesn't. They are simply talking fast to hide their uncertainty from the listener.

Conversely, an expert on a certain topic may choose a slower rate of speech, not because they don't have mastery over the subject, but because they are giving the listener a chance to process the material.

If a person who uses a slower rate of speech seems to be hesitating a lot, however, this may be due to not knowing the material well enough or because they are searching for the right words to use.

Finally, rate of speech communicates nonverbally that the speaker has time to talk (communicating patience) or doesn't have time to talk (communicating impatience). When this happens the speaker can lead the conversation in a way that can leave the listener feeling great or absolutely horrible about themselves.

How do you use this nonverbal tool to your advantage? By monitoring the rate of speech, you will be making sure the listener has an inviting environment to truly listen. Listeners want to feel like they can be there for the speaker and contribute to a conversation. If you would like to build a strong connection between yourself and your child, it is important to monitor how fast or slow you speak.

Silences and pauses

Without a door we would never be able to leave a room. It is the space that is cut out of a room that gives us the ability to go inside or outside the room. We call this space a door.

Without a window we would never be able to feel the weather outside. It is the space that is cut out of a wall that lets fresh air in or out of the room. We call this space a window.

Without a period in a sentence, we would never be able to read. It is the space that is cut out of a sentence that gives us the ability to read and write. We call this space a period.

Without silences and pauses we would never be able to communicate (verbally or nonverbally) with others. It is the space that is cut out of communication that helps structure all the verbal and nonverbal messages we send out and receive from others. We call this space a silence or pause.

Silences and pauses are a necessary part of communicating verbally and nonverbally with others. A buffer of time is needed between the messages you send to your child. Think of it as a pause so they can receive the information properly.

If you are sending rapid fire messages without any pauses, you are not giving the child a chance to understand or act accordingly.

How do you use this nonverbal tool? First, know that a relationship can grow in only two directions: together or apart. When you use silence the way it is intended, you will help your relationship grow with your child.

On the other hand, constantly sending verbal and nonverbal messages of discontent (without any pauses) will cause your relationship to grow apart.

So the next time you are giving a direction to your children, stop and give them a chance to process what you said. Wait quietly, and watch them do what you asked them to do. Also, when you are explaining your thoughts and feelings to them, stop after two or three sentences and check in to see if they understand your statements.

Ask them, "What do you hear me saying?" or "What did I ask you to do?" Wait silently for them to answer completely. You will be surprised to find out that 85 percent of the time, what they heard was not your intended message.

Calmly restate the part of the message they did not understand. Also, give your children a chance to ask a question, or make a relevant comment when appropriate.

Body language (hand gestures and body positioning)

From the time we were born, body language (hand gestures and body positioning) was our first form of communicating with others. For the first two–three years of our life, we literally did not have any words, so our bodies "spoke" for us. We rapidly learned how to use our bodies to speak because our lives depended on it.

Even now we know how to speak and formulate sentences, but our body language is still the first signal we send out to other people. Pay attention when someone is speaking, and you will see that their body language speaks several seconds before words are vocalized!

As a rule of thumb, whatever the mouth does not verbalize, the body will say physically. Not only that, but even when the mouth does speak, our bodies will still supplement the words with body movements, bringing to life our unique form of self-expression.

When we use hand gestures, we are really putting the words we say into action. This serves as a necessary and dramatic effect that emphasizes our communication and current emotional state.

How do you use this nonverbal tool to your advantage? First, start to pay more attention and look at your child's body movements. As you practice this task, you will soon be able to see that you will know what your child is trying to say verbally, sometimes even before your child themselves. Their body will speak first, as they think and search in their word bank for the most effective words to say in that moment.

As you are able to know where the child is going and follow their story, a strong connection will be established between you and your child. Your child (or anyone else) can have no better feeling because being in tune with them is one of the basic human needs. Paying attention to body language is the fastest and most efficient way to understand and connect with your child.

Body Distance

Body distance is the last tool to examine in nonverbal communication. Simply put, body distance is used to take over someone's personal space or give someone personal space. When we are really close to someone physically, it communicates care, concern, seriousness, or someone's safety is in jeopardy. When we are far away from someone physically, it communicates less care, less concern, relaxation, and freedom is permitted.

Usually we see two types of children: those that need their personal space invaded for them to calm down, self-regulate, or do what you ask them to do and those that need extra space for this. Experiment with both to find the particular balance your child has. Sometimes you will need to move closer, and other times you will need to move away.

How do you use this nonverbal tool to your advantage? When you are asking your children to do something and they are not moving, test and see which type of children they are. If they are the "I won't do it till someone is on me" type, move closer (regardless of age).

Note: As a last resort, only use force that is necessary to get the child to move. Lashing out physically is not needed to get your child to do what you ask them to do. If you do lash out, just remember that your children will act with children smaller and weaker than they are the same way you act with them.

Forcing them to follow your instructions will communicate you are serious in that moment. They know you care, even if you are on top of them making them do something they don't want to do.

You are not killing them, like they will try to convince you. The mess will be cleaned in a minute or two, they will forget about it, and they'll go back to playing.

If you find that your children are the "give me fifteen seconds and I'll do it by myself" type, and no danger is involved, move away. (Or if talking to your children is making them more upset, you can move and use silence!).

Even when they throw tantrums, you can still give them space. Just remember it is their loss of control, not yours. As fast as they upset themselves, they can calm themselves down!

When they are calmer, come back. They know you care about them when you are far away. They just want what they want, and they want it now! There is no need to apologize because you let them be for two minutes.

Putting it all together

If this is the first time you've been exposed to these concepts of nonverbal communication, don't feel overwhelmed! Even though it can be a lot to process, take your time with it.

Avoid trying to lump all nine tools together at once or you will frustrate yourself. You will experience a noticeable shift in the dynamics between you and your child by combining two or maybe three of these nonverbal techniques.

With these new tools under your belt, power, flexibility, and leadership skills will be transferred back to where they are supposed to be—in your hands!

Needs vs. Wants

With a better understanding of verbal and nonverbal communication, let us examine the difference between a child's needs and a child's wants. Is there a difference? Yes, there is a very big difference! I would like to take a moment to contrast the two. Let's take a closer look at these concepts.

When we say that a child needs something, what we are really talking about is:

Necessary

Element or

Else

Death

Sound drastic? It is supposed to be! This is because the needed "element" is the difference between life and death for that child!

Here is a list of a child's needs, most of them you'll know:

Food: grains, meats and beans, fruits, vegetables, milk, fats, oils, and sweets (sparingly on the last three)

Water: 70 percent of our body is water; it is vital for survival

Shelter: to protect us from climate and weather changes

Structure: routines, predictability, and to bring order to a world that can be chaotic at times

Unconditional Acceptance (to belong): others are in tune with us as we communicate (Like a radio station, we need others to pick up on our "frequency" for survival.)

Belief in Something: religions, science, rituals, etc.

Clothing: depends on the climate where you live.

When we say that a child wants something, what we are really saying is that:

Wishes that

Are

Nice

To have

Sometimes

Not so drastic? Exactly! This is because children's wants are the wish list that they can really live without. As for a list of a child's wants, simply include everything off the needs list! How can parents balance wants vs. needs? We need to provide all the needs and leverage all the wants. (We will discuss later what leverage is and how to use it).

But like I said earlier, I really want to look more closely at these concepts. With a deeper look, we will see even needs have a deceptive quality about them, and they can become wants.

Food: candy bars, fried chicken, cakes, chips, fast food

Water: Hi C, soda, milk shakes, sweetened ice tea, etc.

Shelter: an eight-bedroom, four-bathroom, three-car garage (when it is only for two people) home

Structure: minute by minute plan for each day or no plan for each day

Unconditional Acceptance: everyone has to agree with us or like us. Everyone must be our friend

Belief in Something: Christianity, Judaism, or Hinduism is the "only way of life" and all others will suffer

Clothing: top of the line, name-brand clothing, shoes, etc.

Throughout the history of man, children have always "wanted what they want, and they want it now!" This is not a new invention created by this generation of children. In fact, this is the way children have always reacted in all generations. Children act this way because they are selfish. In the beginning stages of life, this selfishness is necessary for their survival.

How can a child's selfishness be necessary for survival? If children were not selfish, they would not cry when they were hungry, thirsty, or needed a diaper change. Without these "selfish" cries, the parent would never know what the child needed, and the child would die.

Unfortunately, parents have not been exposed to this information; plus, with technological advancements, basic human needs have been changed into wants (as shown in the section above).

For example, when we were a farming society, did crops grow overnight? No, the family was forced to wait until they were ripe.

As the family waited, parents did not sulk, feel like bad parents, or let their children convince them they were horrible providers because the corn wasn't ready fast enough.

In fact, tantrums would be a useless strategy for children because hysterical crying would not speed up the process. The crops were ready when they were ready.

With great technological advancements, society has drastically changed. In today's world we can actually get what we want and get it now, whatever "it" may be. We do not have to wait five months for crops to grow.

In fact, with the invention of fast-food restaurants, we do not have to wait more than five minutes, and the food is ready! On top of that, there are so many places to choose from, and they are all within a short distance!

Don't get me wrong; technological advancements have been wonderful tools for the human race. These advancements have helped us run operations faster, more smoothly, and more efficiently than ever before!

But bad always comes with the good, and in many respects our technological advancements have played a big role in the breakdown of parent-child and family dynamics. Children want it now, and parents want their children in control now. This is a recipe for disaster.

What can parents do to solve this confusion between a child's needs vs. a child's wants? Simply, parents must provide all needs, and leverage all wants.

How do I leverage my child's wants? Using leverage is like using a car jack. A car jack physically moves the car upwards for us because we cannot lift a car. We push the lever up and down until the car slowly rises.

A child's outburst is like the car, and their wants are like the lever to a car jack. We can literally move the difficult outburst in the direction we lead by using our child's wants as a tool for us. How do we achieve this?

First, be aware that you might feel sorry, embarrassed, or frustrated because you stood your ground. The child will work hard to change your mind. When they try to convince you that their wants are truly a need, simply remember that you are still a caring and concerned parent, whether they get what they want or not. This is true 100 percent of the time! Also, remember the material thing is something they can work for to earn in the future.

Secondly, you can talk with your children about what they wanted even if they are absolutely not going to get it! Where age appropriate you can ask questions about the toy or whatever the desired thing was. You may learn something about your children that you did not know about them as you talk about it. This will help you to be in tune with them—a real need— and open the door for future communication between you and your child.

Finally, if your attempts at talking about it don't work, remain calm. Your child has a shorter attention span than you do! You can always change the subject; tell your child to help you with something (to distract), or simply say, "I'm not talking about the ___ (fill in the blank) anymore" and remain silent and calm.

Since words were not working, stop using them for the time being. Everything will be okay, and you can talk again at a later time (usually in just minutes). Ultimately your child will be learning how to deal with authority and develop coping skills based on what you say and do. You must remain calm, cool, and collected as much as possible, or else they will just follow your out-of-control lead in the future.

Conclusion

Being a parent of a child with ODD is difficult and daunting. But the best way to handle these children and modify their behavior is by actually fixing yourself first. There's a way to thrive in the face of this problem and that's by recognizing that you're going to be much stronger for having encountered and dealt with it. If you're planning to have more children, then, there is no doubt having learned to care for an ODD child will make you a substantially stronger parent. Try to keep this in mind when you feel guilty for showering so much attention on your ODD child while perhaps your other children feel they're not getting adequate attention. This is going to be difficult for them as well. In the context of dealing with sibling jealousy, being able to point to a specified condition, such as "ODD" can be helpful for your other children as they strive to understand the behavior of their sibling and to not take it personally, all while understanding why you, at times, are going to be more patient, more forgiving, and less expectant towards the ODD child. Find ways to reward and recognize your other children. Enlist their support as you seek to care for your ODD child. Explain to them that they, like you, must access a higher realm of patience and compassion, so all of you, as a family, can make it through this difficult situation.

There is no magical drug to take for this disorder, in fact there is no formal pharmaceutical offering recognized specifically for the treatment of ODD. The onus falls back on the parents, teachers, therapist etc. to ensure that the ODD child receives the guidance they need. If parents wish to receive specific ODD training, then there are people such as psychologists, social workers, guidance counselors, spiritual advisors and psychiatrists, who are qualified to provide services for both the parents and the child.

But in order to treat the child, the child must first be understood. The fact that the child's personality is different from everyone else's must be taken into consideration. The parents must remain strong in their dealings with the child; so that they can stand firm, yet at the same time, provide a loving and supportive home environment.

THANK YOU FOR PURCHASING THIS AMAZING MASTERPIECE FOR PREGNANT WOMEN AND FIRST-TIME MOMS IN THE MOMMY'S ANGELS BOOK COLLECTIONS

MOMMY'S ANGELS Book Series was inspired to take the guesswork out of motherhood and childcare. In most cases, from the moment a couple finds out that they are pregnant, their greatest desire is to gather all possible information about pregnancy and motherhood – to avoid being caught up by surprise. As it is often far much better to know what possible problems you may be confronted with, and be prepared and to solve them; as compared to being in the dark.

MOMMY'S ANGELS Book Collections offer some of the most reliable pieces of information that are dedicated to motherhood, many of which have been the true saviors and sure guide for first-time parents. We have received lots of pleasant feedbacks from mothers and, even, fathers who were able to stay calmer reading a book that walks them through each phase of their parenting journey.

You will also find titles that are dedicated to the modern mother who wants to take care of her pregnancy and motherhood, without neglecting her style and femininity.

Like other **MOMMY'S ANGELS Book Series,** the comments, stories, and experiences of pediatricians, psychologists, gynecologists and other mothers like you, contained in this book will help you enjoy the best adventure of your life.

I look forward to hearing your testimonies and awesome feedbacks. **Cheers!!**

MOMMY'S ANGELS
EDITORIAL STAFF
GROW YOUR TODDLER TO THE BEST!

Reviews are not easy to come by.

As an independent staff with a tiny marketing budget, we rely on readers, like you, to leave a short review on Amazon.

Even if it's just a sentence or two!

So if you enjoyed the book, please...

>> Click here to leave a brief review on Amazon.

We are very appreciative for your review as it truly makes a difference.

Thank you from the bottom of our hearts for purchasing this book and reading it to the end.

Printed in Great Britain
by Amazon